Becoming a

It's Never Too Late To Be Who You Might Have Been

by Kathleen Ann Milner

Presented by the Healing Arts Series

Also by Kathleen Ann Milner

Reiki & Other Rays of Touch Healing
ISBN 1-886903-97-2

Tera, My Journey Home:
Alternative Healing
ISBN 1-886903-12-3

Two-Part Historical Fiction Novels with Metaphysical Subplots

Between Two Worlds:
The Story of Henry VIII and Ann Boleyn —
and Her Celtic Heritage
ISBN 1-886903-21-2

Richard III: White Boar
ISBN 1-886903-83-2

In Progress:

Rembrandt: A Novel
ISBN 1-886903-32-8

Cover art — pastel, watercolor, pen & ink
Knock & the Door Shall Open
By Kathleen Ann Milner
P. O. Box 1989, Southern Pines, NC 28388-1989
www.kathleenmilner.com

Chapters

Introduction

Individuals, like John Edwards, who are able to communicate with the departed, are cracking rigid religious views on man's interpretation of the afterlife. The world of spirit holds many possibilities. Some souls become trapped in the labyrinth between the worlds. Other souls travel to the light and then come back to help those whom they loved, or those whom they owe. Angels exist! God works in an infinite number of ways and through many avenues.

The traditional entrance to the Otherworlds is not through a wardrobe but through a tunnel. The Celts used the World Tree. These being 'modern times', students use a variety of means and methods to step through the doorway within the subconscious mind to reach the beautiful place in nature, the beginning of the journey. From this starting point, the Shaman journeys further to facilitate healings, find answers, and creativity. In the process the Shaman discovers her/his own spiritual nature and is afforded the opportunity to become the person s/he was meant to be and live the life that was meant to be lived.

The Shamanic reality is called the Otherworlds. The golden ticket to the Otherworlds is learning how to get there. The key to successful journeywork is understanding the principles governing the Otherworlds and working with enlightened spiritual beings. The ability to demonstrate changes in the physical, and the confirmation of information retrieved defines and separates a true Shaman.

Acknowledgement

This book is dedicated to Vincent, Jordon, Tylor, Alissa, Annalise and all other aspiring Shaman, who know in their hearts that real magic exists.

Thank you to all who have taken the Shamanic class over the years; you have been my teachers, as much as I have been yours. A special thank you to the Shamanic students, who contributed to this book. Your journeys into the extraordinary realities of the Otherworlds lend credence to the exercises herein; your personal development is an exceptional aid to the readers of this book. Your growth is inspirational. You demonstrate that the magic is within us, and arguably easier than purchasing a wand at a shop for wizards in Diagon Alley.

Thank you, Claire Campbell, for an excellent job of proofreading this book!

What Is a Shaman?

Common to all Shaman is a unique manner of meditation through which healings, divination, etc. are carried out. When a Shaman goes within, the Shaman focuses deeper and deeper behind his or her eyes until the Shaman finds an image of her/himself standing in a beautiful place in nature. By focusing on her/his physical form, the left-brain is kept busy in much the same manner as a mantra preoccupies the logical brain in other forms of meditation. With the rational brain engaged, the creative right brain is allowed to explore other possibilities. To aid the Shaman on this journey, someone beats a drum in a rapid, steady tempo, creating an overtone, which seems to harmonize both hemispheres of the brain. In this way, distinctly clear imagery is created. As we live in modern times, an audiotape or CD oftentimes becomes a substitute for the friend with the drum.

The rapid, pulsating, non-varying beat of 205 to 220 beats per minute quiets the active left-brain and the Shaman is plummeted into altered states of consciousness. The Shaman feels dissociated from his/her physical body, thus, allowing her/him to actively participate in the imagery. It is more powerful than virtual reality. Quantum physics agrees that our holographic mind is connected to all aspects of the universal hologram. A Shaman who is channeling sufficient elemental healing energy is able to effectively bring about changes in the hologram simply by altering his/her piece of the hologram.

Shaman means: One who works in the dark. To further aid the clarity of the visual imagery of the inner eye, the Shaman wears a blindfold. This has literally been done for thousands of years, and not just in tribal societies. The Veil of Isis is the Shaman's blindfold. The advanced Egyptian culture considered both the physical and metaphysical aspects of all sciences. For example, astrology and astronomy went hand in hand. We don't typically think of modern inventors as Shaman. However the successful ones, like Shaman, use their creative brain when they are 'deep in thought'.

Unsuccessfully, modern medicine has attempted to find the thinker behind our thoughts. What they found was that the brain is like a radio receiver. The origin of thought or the thinker exists outside of the brain. Creativity is found in the same place. A spark of inspiration from seemingly nowhere lights up the brain in unaware moments. For example, desperately trying to think of the name of a book or an actor, may fail. It is when the matter is set aside and one is engaged in a mindless task that the identifying noun pops into consciousness.

Sometimes revelations happen as we awaken from a night's sleep. Oftentimes, while in the middle of writing a book I will awake with a list of items to add or move from one part of the book to another. When I write I am sometimes aware of warmth coming into a small, narrow channel from the top of my head into the center of my brain. Then phrases, pictures and ideas from somewhere else come into being within the grey matter I call my brain.

Shaman are creative in that they find stimulating new ideas in inward journeys. Rumors have been repeated that Walt Disney and his staff took LSD and found Mickey Mouse waiting for them in Otherworlds. The problem with LSD and other drug-induced states is that the one who journeys is pretty much at the mercy of the drug. There are television commercials that point to one half of the screen and say, "This is your brain!" Then highlight the other half of the screen, which depicts a brain with black holes in it. "This is your brain on drugs!" Drugs leave holes, which cause memory gaps, in the brain. Drugs also leave holes in the aura (energy body around the physical form), opening the door for lower energy forms to enter.

Shamanism as described within these pages is drug-free. Once the journey technique is mastered, the Shaman is emancipated from physical laws, free to go in or out of the Otherworlds at will. Shamanism without drug inducement expands the powers of the mind, opens creative thought processes, brings greater understanding of spirituality, and allows the Shaman to be an active participant in hers/his earthly sojourn. While journeying, the Shaman is coherent and may ask meaningful questions and recall answers.

To reach the place within requires effort. However, if the aspiring Shaman tries too hard, s/he will end up shutting down all visuals. I usually know that I have reached the appropriate place within when I see myself wearing whatever I have on that day. Surprisingly, I remember *that's what I'm wearing today.*

Journeying within is not astral travel. What is astral travel? We all have a spiritual body that looks very much like our physical form. Sleep-time is the soul's awake-time. While we are sleeping, our astral body leaves the physical body through the crown (top of the head), free to wander the astrophysical body of Earth. The astral body is connected to the physical by a silver cord, which is mentioned in many different mysticism and spiritual texts. When death occurs the silver cord is broken and the astral body travels in a vortex of white light to rejoin the greater soul.

People who have had near-death experiences travel upwards towards a loving presence in what they describe as a tunnel of white light. Angels, who tell them that their life's task is not completed, meet them and ask them to return to their bodies. Because the silver cord is not broken they are able to return to their bodies. With the spark of life back in the body there is electricity and the monitors are able to again take readings. If we weren't electrical the hospital machines would not be able to take any readings!

When an individual is in a coma the astral body is also free to roam outside the physical, and again the astral body is connected to the physical form by a silver cord. It's something like Reese Whitherspoon's character in <u>Just Like Heaven</u> but in reality it's a little different. The astral body knows who it is; the conscious mind, more often than not, doesn't remember. Just like some people who have had near-death experiences, sometimes when an individual awakens from a coma s/he is able to repeat overheard conversations verbatim, which occurred in another hospital room or even another city. Movies

4

and books, such as the one mentioned above point out that there is something beyond the physical. There is the possibility that we are more than we think we are.

Some individuals are able to astral travel consciously while in a meditative state. Sometimes, such individuals take my Shamanic class. When it comes time to share after the first exercise, commonly, they will tell the group that a guide came to them shortly after the drumming began and advised them to go within. Not out!

I am sometimes asked if the aspiring Shaman can beat the drum for her/himself. The problem is that as the Shaman journeys deeply within, s/he is unable to maintain the rapid, non-varying drumbeat. One can, however, beat the drum around his or her head for a few minutes at night before going to sleep. This allows the overtone to open psychic centers.

Which brings us to another common characteristic of all Shaman — all Shaman have some form of extraordinary ability. It may be the gift of prophesizing, transformation or healing. Where do these gifts come from? God! The Bible talks about Gifts of the Spirit. It is how these Gifts are used, and where the Shaman focuses his or her attention that is important.

Focusing on the energy within is like the rich man who keeps counting his money. Better to trust that the energy is there for healing, just as the truly rich man trusts that funds will be available when s/he has use for them. The danger of focusing on the energy is that the Shaman may find her/himself on a power trip, just as the rich man who sits on his money will certainly become a miser.

Gifts of the Spirit (healing and prophesy are Gifts of the Spirit) and power (money is a form of power) do not equal spirituality. Rather, Gifts of the Spirit and power are tools given by God for the betterment of others, the planet and oneself. In the end, gifts, wealth and power may be lost but the experience of what was accomplished will last forever. Are those experiences to be the remembrance of energy within, weighty bank ledgers and even larger stock portfolios? Or does the individual choose experiences whereby this world is made a better place?

Shaman have the Gift of Prophecy, intuition or way of listening to the earth. While thousands of people lost their lives in the tsunami that hit the coast of India, many animals headed inland and survived. Why? Because even domestic animals remain close to the Earth and listen to her! Some people are able to sense earth changes, like earthquakes, before there are readings on scientific instruments. The most common way to develop psychic abilities is by meditating or spending time in nature.

Each year, roughly 3,000 people attempt to cross the length of the Appalachian Mountains, which run from Georgia to Maine. In Tennessee and North Carolina they are called the Great Smokies because the recurrent haze gives the impression that they are smoking. The people who attempt the journey are called Through Hikers. While towns along the route are sparse, residents open their arms to the Through Hikers. People, known as Trail Angels, offer assistance or leave bushels of apples along the trail. Damascus, Virginia is the halfway point, where north and southbound hikers are greeted by representatives of outfitting companies, who repair hiking shoes and offer other assistance at no cost. Only several hundred are able to finish. Many discard tents and sleeping bags, preferring to sleep comfortably on the earth. Through their pilgrimage they discover an incredible connection to nature's pulse.

Techniques may also be used to develop psychic abilities. Clairvoyance, meaning to see clearly, is visualizing with the third eye and may be learned by anyone. The third eye is located slightly above and between the two eyebrows. One very old exercise is to hold up a simple object, like a picture or crystal, and stare at it. Then with eyes closed hold the image for as long as possible. Look again. With closed eyes try to hold more of the details of the object. Maintain focused attention. Look again. Try to hold the image in the mind's eye longer. Do this for 5 minutes a day. It takes 21 to 30 consecutive days to build a new skill or change a habit. At the end of 30 days, work with another object. It will not take as long. The last step is to sit with a mirror and afterwards try to hold the image of yourself in your mind's eye.

Another technique for developing good visualization skills is one used by avid readers. Set aside just one hour each day to read a good book. After reading a couple of paragraphs look up. Focus just above eye level, and try visualizing what has just been read.

An old Wicca method for opening the third eye is to stare at a burning candle flame for one minute and then hold the image in the third eye. With this particular technique, if headaches occur, stop using the candle or meditate on the

candle for a shorter period of time. Use
another object instead and go back to the
candle at a later time. There are also
some wonderful guided meditation tapes and
meditation classes.

One way to develop clairaudience or
psychic hearing is to listen to the tone
carried after ringing a Tibetan bell, or
after striking an ordinary bell. Waking up
early in the morning and listening to the
wind can be a powerful experience. The
misnamed Holy Inquisition burned people
alive for this act alone. People who hear
other levels of reality do so not with
their physical ears, but hear about an inch
and a half above the ears at the temple
bone. Psychic messages come into the brain
and are processed through the master
pituitary gland, which is why the sound or
messages seems to be inside the head.

When spirits are seen with the
physical eyes, they appear to move quickly.
So, too, auditory communication is rapid.
Thus, auditory messages do not come in as
complete sentences or long, complex,
flowery paragraphs. Rather, it is usually a
word or phrase that is heard.

Each of the other physical senses has
a corresponding psychic center. It is
possible to smell and taste in other
realities. Sweet smells are an indication
that a highly evolved master or saint is
nearby. When a room goes unexpectedly and
suddenly cold, an earthbound spirit may be
present. Clairsentience is the ability to
feel on other levels. Clairsentience may be
experienced as a shiver down the spine, or
when the hairs on the back of the neck
stand on end. Clairsentience occurs when
the Truth is spoken and every hair on the
arms is left standing on end.

Inner knowing comes in through an open crown chakra. Inner psychic knowing is not in the brain. It is a strong impression in the core of ones being. It is this information that is the most reliable. However, this voice is so quiet that the mind must be free of the incessant chatter and clutter. To check out auditory messages and visual apparitions, simply ask if the message or messenger has come in the Light of Christ. What I tell non-Christians in my classes is that Jesus never claimed to be the only Son of God; he said that we were all capable of becoming sons and daughters of God. In the fourth century, and by only one vote, the Catholic Church voted Jesus divinity. In his day, Jesus was called the Christ because he was so adeptly in tune to the energy of Christ Consciousness.

Bart Ehrman is the Chairman of Religious Studies at the University of North Carolina. He is the author of <u>Lost Christianities</u> and <u>Lost Scriptures</u>. In his latest book, <u>Misquoting Jesus: The Story Behind Who Changed the Bible and Why</u>, he discusses how there are hundreds of errors in the New Testament resulting from translating the Greek texts. Among the inaccuracies are gross intentional errors, which completely change the meaning of some passages. For example, the original New Testament texts in no way supports the Church's later claim that Jesus was divine. Rather, blatant changes altered the meaning in order to support the Church's position. For those people who say that the Bible is a living, growing testimony that may be true. However, the majority of people who read the New Testament want to hear what Jesus had to say.

9

Who was Jesus? According to the original New Testaments, through his healings and miracles Jesus was recognized early on as someone destined to be a great teacher and prophet. He taught the multitudes that the kingdom of God was within everyone and of the goodness of God. He taught his disciples how to heal, sent them into the world to heal and to teach others how to heal. His greatest miracle was the resurrection of his own body. The Mormon Bible is the only one that talks about Jesus' time on the earth after this miracle. The New Testaments are not the only documents that the Church altered. In the original Old Testament, Eve is not Adam's first wife — Lilith is! God never shut mankind out of the Kingdom of Heaven.

It's not that people haven't found comfort and faith in the altered New Testaments, they have! The problem with re-creating God in tainted scriptures, as being strictly in human form with fallibility, is that the Bible becomes a source to justify not only individual prejudices, but great evil as well. Hitler used the Bible to validate the Nazi cause.

The Shaman's extraordinary gifts go with her/him when s/he journeys. It is with these energies and abilities that the Shaman is able to influence the inner environment and hologram. In this way, changes in the Otherworlds have a direct impact on the physical world. The result may be immediate, six months down the road, or a year or more later. By definition a Shaman is one who is able to facilitate changes in the Otherworlds, which transform the physical world.

There is a catch! The Shaman sets his or her general intention before the journey begins and leaves the details to the angels, power animals and spirit guides and other spirit helpers, who journey with the Shaman. The Shaman may always ask questions. However, if the Shaman should try to manipulate the situation or spirit guides, the spirit helpers will depart and the Shaman will be left alone. If the Shaman continues on this downward spiral, very negative spirits will appear.

Do the dead care about the living? It is the question Robert Redford's character asks in An Unfinished Life. Morgan Freeman's character answers affirmatively. These and other questions about the afterlife are being explored in modern theatre, literature and television. One of the last scenes in Harry Potter and the Goblet of Fire describes a way in which the dead help the living after a soul fragment or trauma has been released. Are all spirits able to help? If someone is closed-minded in life, s/he will be equally blocked in the afterlife and be able to offer little in the way of assistance to the living. What happens to Gifts of the Spirit after someone passes? If someone is born with or develops spiritual gifts in life, those gifts will be enhanced in the afterlife. Those gifts may be used to lend a helping hand to those left behind. Saints are those in spirit who possess healing abilities. When people pray to (ask for help; not worship) these saints, many times prayers are answered. Traditionally, the accumulation of miracles that are directly attributed to the intervention of someone who has passed is the evidence that the

Catholic Church examines before bestowing sainthood on a soul that has passed over.

It isn't that previously written poetry and prose have not dealt with the subject of the dead influencing or protecting the living. We have the writing of William Wordsworth, Ralph Waldo Emerson, Henry David Thoreau, William Shakespeare, George Bernard Shaw and even Sir Arthur Conan Doyle's <u>History of Spiritualism</u>. When religious extremes create God in man's image, people lose sight of spirituality and how powerful God is. If one is closed off to ones spiritual nature in life, how will that individual deal with the spiritual afterlife?

WHAT SHAMANISM IS NOT! The following is from Stephen Hassan's <u>Combating Cult Mind Control</u>. As you read through the list, please notice how narrowly defining, rigid and intolerant a cult follower becomes. S/he is in a box without other options. The Catholic Church used these same techniques during the time of the Holy Inquisition. Some radical, right religious groups use them today:

1. The doctrine is reality — the cult's beliefs allow no other interpretations or theories.

2. Reality is black and white — it is good versus evil, plain and simple. No outside group is valid. There is no margin for error.

3. Elitist mentality presumes that they alone are the chosen ones.

4. Group will prevails over an individual's will!

5. Strict obedience to the doctrines.

6. Happiness comes through good performance — behaviors are controlled through shaming and competition.

7. Manipulation through fear and guilt.

8. Emotional highs and lows from great productivity to crashing, due to inadequacies by individuals.

9. Change in time orientation — pre-cult life is bad, very bad!

10. No way out — there is never a legitimate reason for leaving the group.

For a short time, I taught higher-level reading and writing skills at Alverno College. One technique of trying to win people over to faulty reasoning is to initially condemn a terrible condition, and then proceed to be exactly like what one has denounced. Because the undesirable state was so strongly criticized, the reader or listener does not expect the author or speaker to exhibit and then promote the ill-fated qualities but with a different twist. There are politicians who do this regularly. Hitler was but one.

Cult reasoning often defies logic. Logically, if one takes the Bible verbatim and believes that God created Earth in three days, then when the Bible states clearly and without exception that life begins with the first breath and ends with the last, that should be the final Word about when life begins. If the soul entered the fetus then there would be a funeral for a miscarried fetus. There never have been such funerals; not even for a full-term stillbirth. Why? One of the reasons is that psychics who see spirits of the departed and other spirits have always seen the spirit of the unborn outside of the mother. If there is a miscarriage and the fetus is unable to survive, the soul does not enter the body. The soul waits with the angels for another opportunity to be born. God is too good to let a miscarried pregnancy be the only probability for a soul.

After I bred my mare, Duchess, and she returned home, I knew that she was pregnant. As I watched her grazing, with my physical eyes I saw two separate, shiny lights in the aura around her hips. One was blue and the other pink. Interestingly enough, after Mel was born, the veterinarian showed me the afterbirth. There were marks where he had kicked his mom from inside the womb. I remembered on a few occasion seeing one of Duchess' sides heave outwards suddenly and then contract. The veterinarian also showed me a protrusion about the size of a man's thumb on the inside wall of the afterbirth. The ultrasound early in her pregnancy, missed the fact that Duchess was carrying twins. When a mare aborts a fetus, it is reabsorbed back into her body. The pink light was the soul that didn't make it. It is also interesting that Duchess keeps reminding me that she wants to be pregnant again. My psychic inner knowing is that the soul that didn't make it would like to be born as a bay filly with a star on her forehead.

SHAMANISM IS EXACTLY THE OPPOSITE OF CULT MIND CONTROL! Shamanic journeying allows the Shaman to step out of constricted thinking patterns and find creative thought. While journeying in the Otherworlds, the Shaman may return to the physical world at any time. The Shaman is encouraged to ask questions of the angels and spirit guides who accompany her/him while journeying. Shamanism crosses religious barriers.

The Shaman is the one who sets her/his intention before journeying. Intentions may be for healing oneself, others or Mother Earth; finding creative solutions to problems or tasks; finding answers to questions or prosperity. One of the goals of a Shaman, who wishes to get closer to God or Great Spirit, is to release and heal old fears, sorrows, guilt, anger and other destructive emotions. Having a loving heart and clean thoughts impacts any individual's life, and a Shaman's journeys. As Raymond Charles Baker said, "Your life becomes the thing you have decided it shall be."

Before beginning journeywork, the Shaman traditionally honors the 4 directions and 4 elements. Angels and spirit helpers are called in to guide and assist with the journey. The goal or intention of the journey is set. Goals may be as simple as finding a power animal or spirit helpers, or exploring aspects of non-ordinary reality. Common desires are for healing, knowledge, strength, new guides and wealth for the accomplishment of various ends.

In general, there are three worlds that Shaman from different cultures around the world travel to: The Underworld of power animals and nature spirits is actually a beautiful place in nature. Angels and spirits of the departed may be found in the Upperworld. The Middleworld is like Earth's astral body. Michael Harner in The Way of the Shaman refers to this range, which is beyond our ordinary perception, as non-ordinary reality. To our soul, this realm is the real reality, and our lives are the dreamtime through which we learn and grow.

Realities beyond the physical are the same realities that the hero experiences with super-awareness when s/he follows an inner knowing. Courageously and without doubt, the hero does whatever is required in the moment. Non-ordinary feats of bravery and daring are accomplished in altered states. The senses are heightened in what is described as peak experiences. Whole audiences may be drawn into other realities while engrossed in a well-orchestrated play, concert or sports event. When the actors, musicians or players skillfully draw our attention in, the audience focuses intently on the event and physical reality disappears. In this state, the audience is taken into heightened awareness and given glimpses of other realities.

Nothing but the Shaman's own fears and negative thoughts may harm her/him in non-ordinary reality. Nothing! Spirit helpers, guides and angels are available to assist. By an act of sheer will, the Shaman may resist or send anything 'negative' away. Someone else's fearful projections might be easily banished through laughter.

Jesus said that answers are found within. Within each of us is the possibility to work in cooperation with God to create a better life. This inner world has been ventured to in books and workshops on positive thinking, creative visualization, meditation, etc. The Shamanic model offers a structured approach to exploring the inner world. Shamanism is a way to connect with God's creation, as well as with angels and highly evolved beings. Through journeys the Shaman learns how to creatively work with the natural world and explores her/his own unique connection to the Creator. In doing so the Shaman alters life's circumstances for the better. The Shaman begins by honoring God and all of Creation, and then invites all these aspects of the Master Design to aid her/him on the journey within.

INITIATION INTO THE ORDER OF MELCHIZEDEK: The Order of Melchizedek is a healing order of priests and priestess. It is mentioned several times in the Old Testament where Melchizedek is referred to as a King of Salem. It is also stated that Melchizedek ordained Abraham as a priest into the Order of Melchizedek. In other places Melchizedek is called a high priest of The Most Highest God. In the New Testament Christ is mentioned as having ordained a priest into the Order of Melchizedek.

The attunement described in this chapter is the original attunement, which has been given for thousands of years. While there is only one attunement, it is possible to go up in levels by re-attunement or through life's experiences. Levels within the Order of Melchizedek are expressed in double-digit numbers. It was said that Jesus was at level 77 when he began his ministry. Groups that have misused the energy of the Order of Melchizedek have lost it. These include the Jews, the Catholic Church and the

Mormons. The Mormons also lost the golden tablets with ancient Hebrew writing inscribed on them, which were found in Palmyra, New York.

The information on these golden tablets stated that Jesus performed his greatest miracle after his crucifixion — he raised his own body from the dead and then walked the earth. Afterwards, Jesus and some of his followers sailed to the New World. It was also 2,000 years ago, when White Buffalo Calf Woman, who brought spiritualism to the tribes and nations, appeared to Native Americans.

So that all of the workshop participants might have the benefit of channeling healing energy in the Otherworlds of the Shaman, the Order of Melchizedek is given at the beginning of the class. Seven people are attuned at a time. During the initiation into the Order of Melchizedek, the circle that the initiates and initiator stand in, and the spiral that is created by their arms are like symbols, but they are not written symbols. In order to pass the energy of the Order of Melchizedek on, the initiator must be channeling the energy of the Order of Melchizedek. S/he must also be able to hold ceremony or hold Spiritual energy for a group.

The initiation begins with the instructor and initiates standing in a circle. The initiator places her/his right hand, palm down, into the center of the circle. Beginning with the person to the left of the initiator, s/he places her/his right hand on top of the initiator's hand in the same manner. This is repeated around the circle, one by one, in a clockwise

18

direction. When this is completed the person to the left of the initiator places her/his left hand, palm down, on top of the stack of hands in the center of the circle. This continues in a clockwise motion until everyone's left arm and hand are joined in a spiral. The initiator places her/his left hand on top.

The initiator calls upon the priests and priestesses of the Order of Melchizedek and the Priest Melchizedek. Other higher beings, such as, the Fathers of Abraham, Lords of Light and Ascended Masters, may also be called upon. The initiator then says, "Please initiate us into the Order of Melchizedek now!"

When the initiator feels energy in her/his brain, s/he is reminded to tell the group, "Feel the expansion in your brain." As the initiation takes place, initiates feel an expansion in their heads.

When the initiator feels a sensation in her/his lower legs and feet, s/he is reminded to tell the group, "Feel a tingling energy in your lower legs and feet as the energy is being grounded."

The column of Light in the middle of the circle encompasses the group as the individual members are being initiated. Those who have already been initiated may choose to repeat this initiation, as it is possible to go up in levels with each attunement. When people who have received the initiation repeat the initiation, healing energy in the circle may be sent through the circle and into Earth.

When the initiation is completed, the initiator steps back, inviting everyone else to do the same. Starting with the person on her/his left, the initiator walks around the circle and pauses at each initiate. Placing her/his hands on the shoulders of each initiate in turn, the initiator speaks the traditional words, "___(first name)___, thou art a priest(ess) after the Order of Melchizedek forever."

This initiation connects each initiate with the Ascended Masters and the Divine Plan for Mother Earth. It opens etheric healing channels and offers a foundation for all healing work the initiate does. Those stuck in their own agenda are not open to anyone else's possibilities — not even God's. These individuals close themselves off to receiving the initiation into the Order of Melchizedek.

EXPERIENCE OF JOAO RAMOS OF PORTUGAL: During the initiation I saw white, bright light. In the middle of the light came a golden light. I felt the energy in front of my head.

EXPERIENCE OF ANDRE BEUKERS OF THE NETHERLANDS: The first time I was not grounded and we turned counterclockwise. The second time, I was grounded and steady, and we turned clockwise.

EXPERIENCE OF BOTH HANNI BLOMBERG AND LENA LIDMALM, BOTH OF SWEDEN DURING THE INITIATION INTO THE ORDER OF MELCHIZEDEK: I saw a bright light with a black spot in the middle of it. Then I realized it was a large eye looking at me. It only lasted for a moment.

INSTRUCTOR: A large, single eye, especially a floating eyeball, is considered a sign that God is watching out for the individual who sees it.

We Do Not Walk This World Alone

Native Americans in colonial days viewed the white man's lack of connectedness to the natural world as a disconnection from Great Spirit or God. Today, Native Americans joke that the white man has 3 directions — sunrise, sunset and high noon. Through honoring Great Spirit through His creation, Native Americans realized the existence of seven directions - north, south, east, west, above, below and within. Seeking within (the seventh direction) is what Jesus recommended. How we develop the seventh direction determines the quality of our afterlife.

The other six directions are a heightened awareness of the physical world. When we pass over these six directions do not exist, as we know them on this earth plane. Instead, we are encompassed with the love and knowledge that though we are individuals and always will be, we are all connected and a part of All There Is.

While in physical body, seven directions give us insight as to what an all-inclusive sensation is like. It is a part of the Shamanic experience, in that it helps the Shaman to expand outside of her/himself; to see from another point of view and get above the situation. Perception is a large part of being able to co-create, which by its definition means that it takes two. The Shaman works within God's Divine Plan; if s/he doesn't, Holy

Spirit leaves and negative forces take over.

Before journeying within or doing any ceremonial, divination or healing work, a Shaman sets up an altar honoring the 4 winds, 4 directions, 4 seasons and 4 elements. All of the native tribes, wise women of Europe, and Celts understood this power. Sounds easy? Well, humans have managed to complicate the matter.

We are all in agreement on where north, south, east and west lie, thus the 4 directions are easy. The quality of the different winds is relatively simple — it's a matter of where you live. For example, north of the equator the north wind is blustery and the south wind is blistering. South of the equator it is the opposite - north wind is blistering and the south wind is blustery. Consider this - not everyone who lives on this planet receives their weather from the west. Where weather comes from influences the quality of the winds.

The 4 seasons become slightly trickier. The general consensus being that the east is the dawn, the beginning of the day — thus, it represents the spring. West is the sunset, the end of the day — thus, it represents autumn. In order to go clockwise around the wheel, south represents summer and north is symbolic of winter. Why clockwise? Because it is a motion of 'adding into'! Counterclockwise is a motion of release. The next time you happen to attend a Catholic funeral, notice that the priest walks counterclockwise around the casket to release the soul.

In which quadrant each of the 4 elements belongs is outright confusing. Unfortunately, the tribes and the wise women all used different elements in different directions. This is regrettable because if everyone used the same elements in the same directions then ceremonial energy would be stronger.

There are some things that we may ask of God for which we will receive an almost immediate answer. One of these is to ask God for the Truth, *knock and the door shall be opened.* Interestingly enough, individuals on the religious extremes (any religious extreme) refuse to ask. If the question is not presented, how can we fault God for not providing the answers? To hear the Truth, however, it is necessary to quiet the noisy chatter in the brain, and pay attention. Answers and inspiration come in subtle ways.

Curious as to which direction the 4 elements belonged, I asked God. You may do so as well. Here is the answer that I received: The **east** is traditionally known as representing the spark of creation. Many prosperous people have successfully utilized the dawn, an in-between time just before the sun rises above the horizon. Dawn is a time to silently ponder or plan the day. The first light is like that sudden, unexplainable inspiration from nowhere. Spark is a quality of **fire.**

Bibles state that God's Spirit is within everything. Native spiritualism goes a step further and recognizes that God has put His creation here on earth to help us on our journey home. Each of the animals brings a special gift to humanity. Porcupine (innocence) or coyote (laughter) are often depicted in the **south** of Native American medicine wheels. Innocence and laughter are emotional qualities, which are both characteristic of **water**.

White buffalo (wisdom) is often in the **north**. Wisdom is a quality of **air**. The north position at a table, circle or conference is the position of authority.

By elimination, earth is in the west. Bear, horse or another animal of girth, whose footsteps move the **earth**, are typically in the **west**. Dusk is another in-between time and opportunity to meditate, reflect and be thankful for the day. Introspection and prayer are two other qualities of earth. The Lakota Sioux and the Great Iroquois Nation used this particular placement of the 4 elements in the 4 quadrants.

A simple altar on a red cloth (red to ground the energy) may be set up on a small table or large, flat stone. A candle is placed in the east, a vessel of water in the south, a rock or crystal in the west and a knife with a white handle or feather in the north. (Feathers cut through the air.) In the center the Shaman and her/his students might place something that is theirs. Or class members might like to write out petitions, setting them in a bowl in the center of the altar.

Before calling in the energies, the room may be cleared with sage or with the drum. Michael Drake's drumming audiotape begins with a drumbeat of top-bottom-center, which causes the drum to sing out, "Go Away!" Moving counterclockwise around the outside of the circle of the group while drumming counterclockwise around the drum is another way to release unwanted, heavy, dark energies. Oftentimes, even beginning Shamanic workshop participants feel negativity leaving the room and themselves.

When the room and the participants are cleared, it is time to call in the energy. Michael Drake's drumbeat of top-center-bottom rings out, "Come To Me!" The Shaman might also beat around the drum in a clockwise motion while calling in spiritual forces. Chanting in the energies, like the droning of a drum, sets up a strong vibration.

The following is based on the Native American 20 Count, whereby the Shaman calls in all aspects of God's Creation and the Creator Her/Himself. Why this dual aspect of God? Native Americans saw God as having both masculine and feminine aspects. What evidence is there that God is both masculine and feminine? The Bible states that we are created in God's image, if God wasn't also feminine then women would not be here. Nature is also created in God's image, which means that God is present in nature. The Victorian, puritanical, or extreme right version of God as a vengeful old man is the opposite of the Truth.

Brenda Davies asked me to give a one-day, introductory Shamanic-experience workshop. While everyone sat in a circle, I called in the energy one group at a time. After each category, the workshop participants were given an exercise so that they could experience firsthand some aspect of what had just been called in. Afterwards, everyone had an opportunity to share her/his experiences. Readers may want to try to meditate on the exercises to see what insights might come.

25

The first to be called are the elemental rays emanating from Source, which all Shaman, wise women, saints and other healers have used since the beginning of time. A Shaman who draws the energy with her/his hand or with a stick on the ground, will go from north to south and then from east to west. With that in mind, here is how the 4 elements may be called in:

CALLING IN OF THE ELEMENTAL RAYS: *I call upon the Tibetan Masters. I call upon all who have used the elemental rays who have come before and who will come after me, who have come in the Love of Christ and the Light of Buddha. I call upon the core and the Source of the elemental rays and the ancient ones. Air, air, air! Water, water, water! Fire, fire, fire! Earth, earth, earth! Spirit, spirit, spirit! Air, air, air! Water, water, water! Fire, fire, fire! Earth, earth, earth! Spirit, spirit, spirit! Air, air, air! Water, water, water! Fire, fire, fire! Earth, earth, earth! Spirit, spirit, spirit!*

EXERCISE: The circle is organized in such a manner that equal numbers of people are clearly sitting in each of the 4 directions. Those sitting in the north begin by chanting, "Air, air, air!"
Those in the south follow by chanting, "Water, water, water!"
East is next! "Fire, fire, fire!
West is last! "Earth, earth, earth!"
Then the whole group chants, "Spirit, spirit, spirit!"

The group repeats the sequence maybe five to ten times, or even more. The energy builds with each round. Afterwards, the participants are asked to feel the energy and then to breathe the healing energy into the major etheric energy centers of the body, which are called chakras. If everyone does the same exercise at the same time, the energy is stronger. It also helps to visualize oneself while doing the exercise and watch the healing coming in and toxicity removed. If the participant has questions, s/he may ask the angels or spirit helpers:

Beginning with the top of the head, or the crown chakra. Breathe healing energy into the **crown**. Exhale and breathe out toxins. Repeat two more times.

Breathe healing energy into the **third eye**. Exhale and breathe out toxins. Repeat two more times.

Breathe healing energy into the **throat**. Exhale and breathe out toxins. Repeat two more times.

Breathe healing energy into the **heart** chakra, which is over the sternum. Exhale and breathe out toxins. Repeat two more times.

Breathe healing energy into the **solar plexus** or stomach area. Exhale and breathe out toxins. Repeat two more times.

Breathe healing energy into the **naval**, which is our connection to our Spiritual Mother or Goddess. Exhale and breathe out toxins. Repeat two more times.

Breathe healing energy into the **creative** or 2nd chakra, which is located at the belly. Exhale and breathe out toxins. Repeat two more times.

Breathe healing energy into the **root chakra**, which is located at the base of the spine. Exhale and breathe out toxins. Repeat two more times.

At this point, healing energy has been brought into the front chakras and down the etheric energy line that runs through the middle of the body. The front and back chakras are attached to this line of energy. Now it is time to bring the healing energy up the spine through the back chakras, which are opposite the front chakras. This exercise does not awaken the kundalini. The kundalini energy will rise up the spine when all of the chakras and issues are clean and resolved.

Breathe healing energy into the **back 2nd chakra.** Exhale and breathe out toxins. Repeat two more times.
Breathe healing energy into the **small of the back.** Exhale and breathe out toxins. Repeat two more times.
Breathe healing energy into the **back solar plexus** chakra. Exhale and breathe out toxins. Repeat two more times.
Breathe healing energy into the **back heart** chakra. Exhale and breathe out toxins. Repeat two more times.
Breathe healing energy into the **back of the neck.** Exhale and breathe out toxins. Repeat two more times.
Breathe healing energy into the **back of the head.** Exhale and breathe out toxins. Repeat two more times.
Breathe healing energy into the **crown** chakra. Exhale and breathe out toxins. Repeat two more times.

EXERCISE: As a variation of the above exercise, go through the entire sequence once and spend time visualizing the cleansing of the organs and glands that are located behind or next to each chakra. As the energy is brought up the spine, visualize the vertebrae or disks in the spine.

EXERCISE: Alter the meditation by silently repeating the sound "So" with each inhale breath, and "Hum" with each exhale.

EXPERIENCE OF JOHN OSTROWSKIS OF SHEFFIELD, ENGLAND: Dear Kathleen, I am going through an incredibly interesting time at the moment. Seems like I'm at a time when change/transformation is just going ahead easily without too much resistance. Recently, I started doing a meditation exercise that you described in Reiki & Other Rays of Touch Healing — breathing in 'So' and out with 'Hum' through the chakras. Well, I was at a meditation workshop on the weekend and had a deep experience of the Universe breathing into me with the same resonance. In doing the So/Hum exercise yesterday, rather than the words 'So' and 'Hum', I heard a distant Gregorian-type chant from a higher being intoning the 'So' 'Hum'. (Don't know if the being was intoning the Universe or the other way around, or if they were the same thing.) It then felt as though the Universe caught me listening and started signing into my chakras. Doing the So/Hum exercise at home before the meditation workshop obviously started opening the doors. Seem to be attracting stuff that's right for me to move on, with the pivotal point being the healing I received from you in the Creativity Workshop. So, thanks!

CALLING IN THE FATHERS OF THE OLD TESTAMENT AND MELCHIZEDEK: *I call upon the priests and priestesses of the Order of Melchizedek! The Priest Melchizedek! Ancient ones! Watchers! Seers! Fathers of Abraham!*

EXERCISE, WHICH MIGHT BE A GUIDED MEDITATION OR JOURNEY: See yourself clearly in your mind's eye standing in a beautiful place in nature. Ask the Priest Melchizedek to come and take you to a place of healing. You may ask questions.

EXERCISE: Stand in a circle with those who have been initiated into the Order of Melchizedek. Interlock arms and hands as if commencing with the attunement. Call upon the priests and priestess of the Order of Melchizedek to send healing into Earth.

CALLING IN THE ANGELS: *Angels of the Violet Fire, Angels of the Violet Fire, Angels of the Violet Fire! Angels of transformation and protection, power and love, beauty and harmony, magic and healing, abundance and prosperity, angels of justice, mercy, grace, forgiveness, compassion, truth, joy, inspiration, be here now!*

Evidence that people believe in **angels** dates back thousands of years. Angelic reliefs were discovered in Mesopotamia. Angels were found described on Sumerian cuneiform cylinders and clay tablets — the oldest writings found on earth. Ancient Mayans carved angels on the Acropolis of Ek Balam in the Yucatan. Angels may be found in Jewish, Christian and Islamic Bibles and teachings.

Some people attribute all apparitions to either being Jesus, Mary or an angel. However, there is a distinct group of beings, called angels, who seem to have evolved on another plane of existence. There are countless stories of angels intervening and helping people. When the silver cord is cut and the astral body is set free to rejoin the greater soul, angels are present to guide the personality to heaven or the Upperworld.

EXERCISE, WHICH MAY BE DONE IN A JOURNEY OR GUILDED MEDITATION: Call upon the Angels of the Violet Fire. Feel their distinctive energies of transformation. Whatever there is in your life or body that you wish to be altered, give it to the Angels of the Violet Fire. You may ask questions of the angels. Watch the transmutation and the resulting renovations.

CALLING IN OF THE ARCHANGELS: *I call upon the celestial angels and archangels — Michael, Gabriel, Uriel, Raphael, Jophiel, Zadkiel, Metatron, Sandelphon.*

EXERCISE, WHICH MAY BE DONE IN A JOURNEY OR GUIDED MEDITATION: Metatron and Sandelphon are the only archangels whose names do not end in "iel". They are twins and were once fallen angels, who managed to work themselves back up to 'archangel status'. Their gift is inspiration and hope to humanity. See yourself clearly in your mind's eye standing in a beautiful place in nature. Call upon Metatron and Sandelphon. Ask them, "How did you manage to climb up from the depths of despair?" . . . Ask them, "What inspiration might you offer me?"

CALLING IN OF THE GREAT WHITE BROTHERHOOD FROM THE GREAT WHITE LODGE: *I call upon the Great White Brotherhood from the Great White Lodge! Jesus, Moses, Mohammed, Blue Star, Buddha, Thoth, Krishna, Sai Baba, Babaji, Senat Kumara, Serapis Bey, El Moray, Tamarasha, So Se Gung, Muktananda, Straight Arrow, Yogananda, John Paul I, Quetzelquatal, Osiris, Ptah, Pan, Genesh, Master Mary, Mary Magdalen of the Veil, the Black Madonna, White Buffalo Calf Woman, Quanyen, Locksheme, Kahli, Amagee, Athena, Isis, Asatarte, Hagati, Demitra, Diana, Hava, Ostara, Sekhemet, Guadelupa, Hathor, Nepthus, Bast, Inanna!*

The Great White Brotherhood in this respect is not an earthly club or fraternity, but an assemblage of avatars. Others classified under The Great White Brotherhood, such as Thoth, once lived an extraordinary life, making exceptional contributions. Others, like the Black Madonna, are personifications of a larger consciousness. There are three churches in St. Mere Eglises, France that are connected to the Black Madonna. Once a year, gypsies from all over Europe come to this place to take the Black Madonna into the ocean and ask for her blessings.

Another way to explain the Black Madonna is that everything that has DNA has a consciousness. Earth, unlike the other planets in our solar system, is a living planet. Anything that has life has a spiritual consciousness. The Black Madonna is the human personification of the spirit that embodies Mother Earth. Should Earth die that spirit will move on. Many societies honor Mother Earth and the Black Madonna so that Earth may flourish, and in the hopes that gifts may be bestowed upon those who are respectful of the Earth and God's creation.

There are truths and eminent teachers (or Bodhisattvas) in all of the great religions. There are also universal archetypal energies. An example of this is the Holy Kabbalah, which may well have its roots in Egyptian mythology. In the Kabbalah, Keter is representative of God, The Great God Almighty or Yod. Keter is the Divine Intelligence, which sees the hidden patterns that form the ideal plan. We as humans not only fail to see order amidst chaos, but we have trouble finding our own life's plan. Keter represents that initial spark of creation or insight that comes from seemingly nowhere. As humans are a microcosm of the Great Macrocosm, on a microcosmic level Keter represents the thinker behind our thoughts.

From Keter the sephirot (archetypal constructs) are sent out. It is as though Keter's spark of inspiration has the ability to trigger a series of events. This occurs in our lives when we act on that 'gut feeling' and take a chance. The first sephirot are Bina (wisdom) and Hochma (intelligence). Hochma is sometimes portrayed as impregnating Bina. Dwatt is the eleventh sephirot, who represents on a microcosmic level the connection between the thinker and the thought. On a macrocosmic level Dwatt is the link between our thoughts and the Creator. Dwatt reminds us to watch what we say and think.

Bina and Hochma give rise to the other sephirot. In order for anything to happen there must first be thought and intention. After thought, emotion is added into the mix. Hesed (love) and Gevurah (power) may operate individually or together. When they operate in unison, the relationship between Gevurah and Hesed becomes dynamic. Together they form Tiferet (beauty and harmony). Tiferet is the stabilization of opposing forces and is expressed in artistry, ethics, nature and healing.

Netza and Hod take these same emotions and archetypal constructs to a level of understanding that is beyond our lives on a 3-dimensional planet. Netza is eternity! Hod is majesty! When Netza and Hod operate together they form Yesod. Yesod is the stability that comes when all aspects and talents of an individual soul are allowed to play out in relationship to the Whole.

Malkhut bridges the gap between intellectual understanding and action. Malkhut is also the link between our conscious reality and the reality of our own higher self. Malkhut acts as a bridge between heaven and earth, in much the same way as eagle bridges the gap between heaven and earth in Native American spirituality. In the Kabbalah, Malkhut is the lost sephirot and feminine in nature. Perhaps, Malkhut suffers when the patriarchy becomes oppressive.

Meditating on any of the above aids in understanding, and brings these special attributes into form. For example, meditating on Malkhut or eagle, one might ask for prayers to be manifested or, *what is the direction my life is to take now?* As most people who come to my workshops or sessions are looking for a change in their lives, I picked the Hindu elephant-headed god, Genesh, for the workshop attendees to work with. Genesh is the archetypal energy of new beginnings, as well as the ability to break through blockages or old patterns in order to create fresh starts.

EXERCISE, WHICH MIGHT BE A GUIDED MEDITATION OR JOURNEY: See yourself clearly in your mind's eye standing in a beautiful place in nature. Ask the angels to guide you to your path of life. Are there any blockages up ahead? Ask Genesh to remove the obstacles. Are you coming to a crossroad? Ask Genesh to open a higher, more productive, more meaningful, more joyful course.

EXERCISE, WHICH MIGHT BE A GUIDED MEDITATION OR JOURNEY: See yourself clearly in your mind's eye standing in a beautiful place in nature. Ask the Black Madonna or Earth Mother to come to you. She is beautiful and richly colored like the Earth. Ask her, "How might I assist the Earth?" Ask her, "Please help me to be the person I was meant to be; to live the life I was meant to live."

CALLING IN OF THE SAINTS: *I call upon the saints! Joseph, Jude, Christopher, Lucy — help me to see clearly, Theresa, Patrick, Sheila, Bridget, David, Elijah, Martin — open my psychic abilities, Dorothy, Clare, Francis - protect the animals, Blaze — heal my throat, Elizabeth, Ann, Catherine, Thomas Becket, Andrew, Anthony, Swethen, Germain, Bernard Casey, Saint Rita!*

All of the saints have a particular attribute that they are famous for. A few examples are given above. For almost 2,000 years, the Church has posthumously bestowed sainthood on an individual if miracles were attributed to her/him after death. The examination process was involved and extensive research and corroborative evidence was required. Sainthood was not granted because someone lived an extraordinary or pious life. Some but not all of them were healers in their own lifetime. Praying to a saint is not worshiping the individual as a god or goddess. Praying to a saint is simply asking for help. For example, there are many people who know that a deceased loved one is around and they ask that soul for help. The following example of a saint comes from <u>Richard III: White Boar</u>. As you read, practice visualization skills. After each paragraph elevate your focus to just above the horizon. Remember and envisage what was just read.

Richard and George had both heard about Canterbury. Canterbury was the most popular shrine in England, nay, all of Europe. Its importance as a major pilgrim destination dated back to 1170. Thomas Becket, Archbishop of Canterbury, had been Henry II's friend and protégé, but Henry discovered too late that Becket had a backbone. Becket refused to allow the Church, her property and riches to be subordinate to Henry II's control. After years of struggle between the two men, Henry II publicly proclaimed, "Will no one rid me of this low-born cleric?"

Four knights, loyal to the King, took up the challenge. They made no secret of their intent to kill Becket. The Archbishop was warned, but he preferred to face the inevitable in the sanctuary of Canterbury Cathedral, rather than be killed in some obscure location. On December 29, 1170, the knights arrived at the cathedral. When Becket refused to leave they tried unsuccessfully to manhandle him. Richard de Brito dealt the fatal blow by slicing off the top of Becket's head with his sword. Shock and horror reverberated throughout England and the Continent. Henry II was forced to have the knights executed, but that was not enough! Henry relinquished all attempts to subjugate the Church to the State's authority. That was not enough! Three and a half years after Becket's death, Henry II was compelled by Pope Alexander III to do penance. Henry showed up at the Cathedral shoeless and wearing sackcloth, to be flogged next to Becket's casket.

Immediately after Thomas Becket's death, miracles began to occur for those who prayed at Becket's coffin, located in a crypt in the basement. Unexplainable wonders and healings led to Becket's canonization on February 21, 1173. Pilgrims from all over Europe prayed at Canterbury for Saint Thomas Becket's intervention. They left donations, from a few simple coins to exquisite jewels, jewelry and gold. Canterbury's pilgrim traffic superseded that of Winchester Cathedral where the shrine of Saint Swithun and the tomb of Alfred the Great resided.

In 1220, Becket's remains were ceremoniously moved up to the ground floor of the Cathedral. Behind the high altar a gorgeously prepared tomb laid waiting. It was there that Becket's last resting place prevailed in spite of the fact that more miracles occurred when his remains were in the basement.

EXERCISE — GUIDED MEDITATION: Focus on a particular problem or body pain that you would like help with. Ask a saint to come in and help.

CALLING UPON THE LIGHT WORKERS: *I call upon the Light workers, Kathryn Cullman, Edgar Cayce, Thomas Alva Edison, Einstein, Tesla, Mozart, Beethoven, Dr. Bach, Mendel, Jim Gore, Chief Black Hawk, Chief Sitting Bull, Eleanor Moore, Audrey Hepburn, Michael Landon, Anne Frank, Elizabeth Ann Seton, Jackie Kennedy, Jack Kennedy, White Horse, Tiba, Princess Diana!*

The Light workers have not received official offers of sainthood by the Catholic Church. The Light workers I call in are personalities that I had a meaningful interaction with either while they were alive or in spirit. For example, while I never met Jackie Kennedy, she is the spirit who helps me edit. While most of her time is spent with her daughter and grandchildren, I believe that it is her spirit, who helps revise, rework, amend and change my books for the better. As an affirmation, once I saw Jackie with my physical eyes, standing at my computer.

EXAMPLE: Shortly after Jackie Kennedy's son's plane went missing, she brought John's spirit to me. I don't often see with my physical eyes, especially during the day. However, I could see John's energy pattern and the distinctive wave to his hair. Talking with spirits, who are in another dimension, is not like carrying on an earthly conversation. Rather, it is like getting impressions or hearing phrases or having an inner knowing in the core of my being.

What Jackie and John conveyed to me was that John could have gone to the Light but his wife, Caroline, was caught between the worlds. Apparently, while Caroline's sister was in the back and unable to see the fast-approaching ocean and inevitable crash, Caroline had a perfect view and died in a state of intense fear. After death, Caroline's sister went to the Light, but Caroline's terror was keeping her earthbound, or in this case, waterbound. John felt responsible and stayed behind to help her. I explained to John that he would not be able to help Caroline in his present state. He would have to go to the Light first and then come back to help Caroline. If he wanted to do so, he could come back to me and I would help him. After consulting with his mother and the angels, who were with him, John left in the Light.

It wasn't many weeks later, when John returned and made his presence known. It so happened that three of my students were in my home that afternoon. We were all honored to be of assistance.

From my living room I asked the angels to open the vortex of Light over the Atlantic Ocean where John's plane went down. Then the four of us built up healing energy and sent it to Caroline. We did this several times. Finally, the angels and John were able to get Caroline out of the water. With one more healing effort, Caroline went to the Light.

Then I asked if there were any other souls who wished to make their transition at this time. A figure bound in chains and wrapped in black entered the room. A very little, dark-haired boy preceded him. It was John as he looked when J.F.K. died.

I knew several things all at once. The heavy fetters and black mantel did not belong to Jack Kennedy. Someone or a small group of people had taken the President's brain and worked black magic to capture the essence of J.F.K.'s personal magnetism and power for their own use. (It is possible to do black magic of this kind before the soul has made its sojourn into the Light.) As the President had been let down by so many around him, his children were the only ones left that he would have trusted. Before John Jr. was born, events had already transpired that would lead to the President's assassination. Nostradamas, in predicting the deaths of both John and Robert Kennedy, said that while some things could be changed or altered, the murders of the two brothers were inevitable. Well before the first breath that brought the young John Kennedy's soul into his body, he had agreed to die at the time he did. In doing so to help his father reclaim what was his and to go to the Light.

Something made me turn my head. With my physical eyes I saw a large head of Robert Kennedy. In looking back, I believe that the size represented the energy that was required to release J.F.K. The angels surrounded us in silver while we called in healing energy and sent it to J.F.K. With one great single effort, heaven's will and the strength of the angels and spirit helpers, J.F.K. was released from his restraints, regained what was his, and was sent to the Light.

J.F.K. is a very advanced soul, who is now one of many who are helping Mother Earth at this time of her transition into consciousness. J.F.K.'s presence is sometimes felt when we are doing healings for the Earth. As for the younger John Kennedy, another reason he left at the time he did was because he was ready to learn about spirituality.

EXERCISE: As the group sits in a circle, the teacher holds her/his arms and palms of the hands out. S/he asks the angels to please open the vortex of Light. Members of the group are invited to feel the energy change in the middle of the circle. Only the lost souls who are ready to cross over are invited to take the hand of an angel and step into the Light. The first time, the long mantra is articulated slowly. Then it is chanted several times as those who have been trapped between the worlds find an angel's hand, step into the Light and begin to rise upwards. Sometimes, souls need encouragement. So, the teacher might say, "If where you are isn't working for you, why not take a chance and try something different?" Sometimes, souls want to know what it will be like where they are going. So, the teacher tells them, "You will be going to a beautiful place in nature that is beyond comprehension. There the angels will take you to places of healing." In one last effort, the teacher might say, "Last curtain call!"

Chanting the following sets up a droning, like the droning of the drum. The vibration seems to provide earthbound souls a means of getting into the Light:

INSTRUCTOR & STUDENTS CHANT: You are loved, blessed, healed and forgiven! You are loved, blessed, healed and forgiven! You are loved, blessed, healed and forgiven! You are one with your own higher self! Take the hand of an angel! Go into the Light. Go with Jesus, go with Mary, go with Buddha, go with Quan Yen, go with Krishna, go with Kali, go with Mohammed, go with Fatima! Go now! Go with angels, go with the Great White Brotherhood, go with the Saints, go with the Bodhisattvas! Go now! Go to heaven, go to the Light! Go now! Go to peace, light, love, joy, healing, mercy, grace, forgiveness, wonder, inspiration, enlightenment! Go now!

Sometimes, workshop participants feel or see spirits of those they have known or loved step into the passageway that leads to the next world. Sometimes, a large black figure will drop her/his black shroud just before stepping into the Light. The energy from their departure is quite intense; maybe because of the great courage and effort it takes to make a transition of this magnitude. Black shrouds left behind are transformed by Celestial Angels. For those who wish further reassurances, the teacher may call in the transformational color violet, the Violet Flame or the Angels of the Violet Fire. There is no possible danger from any of these spirits because the spiritual parameters were defined from the outset - only those who are ready to go to the Light may enter.

During the session, most people in the group in some way experience the souls who are making their transition. Some see, hear or feel the passage of a soul or souls as they step into the circle. Most earthbound souls look very much as they did in life at the time of their death. Initially, they may not have even realized that they were dead. Some are confused because they have never been told about the in-between place in which they now find themselves trapped! Apparitions oftentimes appear translucent because we are looking from one dimension into another. If a soul has the ability to muster up enough energy, s/he may be seen as solid. Earthbound souls always see themselves as having breadth, height and weight. The physical is always where one happens to be.

One of the big difference between this side of the veil and the next is that on the other side, emotional pain or bad memories cannot be blocked. We will always be physical, mental and emotional. However, in the next dimensions these aspects are upfront. There are no secrets on the other side of the veil. Suicide to escape mental and emotional pain is a waste of effort. It is easier to work out mental and emotional pain on this side of the veil.

An earthbound soul might not have been able to find her/his way to the Light because of unfinished business. It is also possible to be held back because of a lack of understanding of the dying process and spiritual laws. It is possible for the living to hold onto a deceased loved one. To help these particular souls go on, they may need to know that they have permission to leave. Repetition of prayers, chanting a mantra or singing while the soul goes into the Light also creates a resonance that helps the soul move on.

Brown, earthbound spirits carry a heavier load. Their baggage at the time of death involves denser emotions of rage, hatred and greed. Their only garment is oftentimes the crusty brown residue on their form. To the living, these spirits may be troublesome, unseen companions. They might be unpleasant factions in homes, other structures or objects — manmade or natural.

Black spirits are those who committed serious crimes against society and nature. Their sins may include murder, political or judicial corruption, blackmail or the practice of black magic. Black magic on the surface may appear to offer a quick fix; however, everything we do comes back to haunt us for good or bad times the power of ten. While brown earthbound spirits have features, black spirits have none. They have truly lost themselves. These black spirits may be bound to the place where they are held most accountable. This may also be an object. Those who feed off of humanity's fears, sorrows and anger may use the power of the negative emotions of black spirits to wreck further havoc.

There are also demons that may wish to go to the Light. Demons are mentioned in the Bible, but they are not what you might expect them to be! Many demons took form in black magic rituals. Black magicians torture an animal or an innocent. At the point of death, the black magician binds the soul. Through the fear, pain and spell, the soul forgets who s/he is. However, when the black magician dies, the demons s/he created haunts the black magician in the afterlife and through other lifetimes. Many in the circle are shocked to see that as demons enter the Light, they become children.

For the record, exorcisms are different! Rather than asking willing spirits to come into the circle and go to the Light, people go into a haunted environment or offer to assist someone who is possessed. The exorcism may begin by asking the angels to open the vortex of Light and the calling upon of great souls, like Jesus. The repetition of the mantra given several pages ago may be repeated over and over again. In this way, all are given the opportunity to experience God's forgiveness and love. Sandlephon and Metatron might be called in to assist. When this does not work, angels of exorcism and release are called upon to clear the person or location. Even at this point, the soul has the possibility to go to the Light. If, however, they refuse to go to the Light then angels take them to another place. The whole process may take hours. It is highly ill advised and NOT recommended for anyone to invite an entity into her/himself thinking that the group will have an easier time in clearing. There is a process for exorcism included in the last chapter, *Katimbo.*

CALLING UPON THE 4 WINDS, 4 DIRECTIONS, 4 SEASONS and 4 ELEMENTS: *I call upon the 4 winds, 4 directions, 4 seasons, 4 elements! Dazzling wind of the east, I bid you come forth! Bring with you energies of fire! Energies of transformation, illumination, passion, creativity! Lend me your power, lend me your might, bring your magic and healing to my sight! I invoke thee, I summon thee, I call thee forth! I invoke thee, I summon thee, I call thee forth! I invoke thee, I summon thee, I call thee forth!*

Blistering wind of the south, I bid you come forth! Bring with you energies of water! Energies of healing, love, compassion, beauty, and the development of my psychic abilities! Lend me your power, lend me your might, bring your magic and healing to my sight! I invoke thee, I summon thee, I call thee forth! I invoke thee, I summon thee, I call thee forth! I invoke thee, I summon thee, I call thee forth!

Buoyant wind of the west, I bid you come forth! Bring with you energies of earth! Energies of grounding, foundation, introspection and prayer! Lend me your power, lend me your might, bring your magic and healing to my sight! I invoke thee, I summon thee, I call thee forth! I invoke thee, I summon thee, I call thee forth! I invoke thee, I summon thee, I call thee forth!

Blustery wind of the north, I bid you come forth! Bring with you energies of air! Energies of wisdom, knowledge, communication, gratitude! Lend me your power, lend me your might, bring your magic and healing to my sight! I invoke thee, I summon thee, I call thee forth! I invoke thee, I summon thee, I call thee forth! I invoke thee, I summon thee, I call thee forth!

God The Father Almighty in Taoism is an active verb Who is found in nature and in each and every one of us. Most other religions also agree that God's Great

Spirit permeates this world and this universe. In order for any life form to come into being, a spirit must be willing to enter the physical at the time life begins. For humans and animals, the soul enters with the first breath. Where is the proof of these statements? Science has proven that anything that has DNA has a consciousness. The Bible's only explanation of when life begins states clearly that the soul enters the body with the first breath and leaves with the last. Psychics, who are able to communicate with the departed and confirm to the living that personality survives death, will sometimes describe a pet accompanying the diseased.

When we honor nature, others, and ourselves we honor God and become expressions of God. Religions have a tendency to re-create God in man's image; religious extremes go a step further and re-create God according to their particular point of view. Thus, religious fanaticism takes the place of spirituality. Rather, God is multidimensional — if that were not so, our prayers would have no hope of being answered. If God was something apart from this planet then there would be an impenetrable barrier between this world and the next.

One of the problems with extreme religious zeal is that members lose sight of the great power and love of the Creator. Science is the study of the natural laws and an explanation of how God creates. Scientists have been trying to discover what came before the Big Bang, or how God created this universe. So, they came up with a String Theory, but soon there were five string theories when there should only be one. Recently, scientists have discovered what might be described as eleven planes of existence. At the eleventh level are two vastly incomprehensible, great, undulating forces. They are so mighty in scope that whenever these two forces touch, a new universe is created. Each new universe may or may not have physical laws that are similar to our universe.

Within the Universal Consciousness exist four elements — earth, air, fire and water. Within each element are finely tuned rays or vibrations, which may be used for healing and magic. As discussed previously, all healers, wise women, magicians, Shaman, and some saints have knowingly or unknowingly utilized the elemental rays to reconstruct or transform physical reality, which is also made up of earth, air, fire and water.

As God is multidimensional, so is creation. On another plane of existence there are beings called the elementals. They are different from the elemental rays of healing and magic. Elementals take form in what the Greeks referred to as the Sylphs of the air, Gnomes of the earth, Salamanders of the fire and Undines of the water. The elementals have been loved, misunderstood and feared. However, one thing is for certain, they have been observed throughout history by all of the old cultures. In Ireland they were called the Wee People.

The Menehunes, the 'little people' or elementals, were Kauai's first residents. Elementals have different names in different indigenous cultures around the world. They sometimes appear in miniature human form. The elementals live in another dimension or what some call a parallel universe. When an individual's psychic centers are clear and have been developed, and the elemental so choose, people see them. When I was in Kauai, I saw the elementals twice as rich, earthy-colored balls of energy. When I asked if the natives of Kauai had similar experiences, I was told that if they had, they were not talking. Too much fear had been instilled by Christian indoctrination.

In Shamanism the Underworld is a wondrous realm inhabited by the elementals, nature spirits, divas and power animals. These are considered to be Spirit Helpers, which the Shaman uses for divination, healing and other spiritual work. Henry Ford and George Washington Carver worked with these intuitive forces to bring about new innovations and inventions.

EXERCISE: As a gesture, the teacher opens the window and invites the elementals to come into the room. The group is invited to welcome these beings. The teacher asks the group, "Think of a question that requires a yes or no answer. In a minute, you will silently ask the question of the elementals. If you feel a scratch on the top of your head, it means that the answer is yes. If your nose is pulled, the answer is no."

Some people feel the response right away; others do not! So, the group is invited to think of another question and ask the elementals for the answer. By about the fifth question, most people begin to feel the answer. When the answer is surprising and turns out to be correct, the workshop participant knows that something else exists outside of the immediate physical world.

EXAMPLE: In the fall of 2005, I met a dozen or so people from Belgium and The Netherlands in Hoogeloon, which is in the southern part of The Netherlands. Hoogeloon is famous for sightings of gnomes; there is even a statue of a gnome in the city. Walking trails and carriage rides carry people, who are hoping to encounter a gnome or two.

Even the disbeliever sees why, if there are such things as gnomes, that they would prefer Hoogeloon. Large, hardwood trees line the lanes and roads. Rather than tilling all of their land, farmers leave groves of trees. The smell of nature is in the air. For the believer, this is a hopeful sign that the elementals are around.

Our group started out standing with our backs against the trees in a wooded public area. I invited the group to concentrate upon one chakra at a time, and by a sheer act of will, allow the chakra to merge into the tree. Then allow the tree to clean the chakra. On a physical level, trees turn carbon dioxide into oxygen; on a metaphysical level, trees turn our 'stuff' into positive energy.

We ended up standing or sitting with our backs to the trees for well over two hours. Everyone in the group had the distinct feeling of the gnomes working on their issues or pains. Some people saw the gnomes in their third eye, others heard the gnomes, but everyone felt better before leaving. When I concentrated within, I saw the gnomes not as colored balls of light, but gnarly, resembling an old oak.

At the end of the day, one man said that he felt his heart charka go into the tree, but became afraid. His heart chakra came back into his body. When another chakra went into the tree, his fear stopped him.

I can totally sympathize with this man. A long time ago, I remember waking up in the middle of the night and seeing a life-size, golden, glowing statue of Saint Theresa, the Little Flower, hovering above my bed. I was so frightened that it seemed as if my heart was beating outside of my body. I asked three times for it to go away; after the third time it left. I didn't know then that the best thing to do under these unusual circumstances is to call on Buddha or Christ or another higher being to help by asking three times, "In the love of Buddha and the Light of Christ, if this is for my highest and best interest, please stay, otherwise go away and stay away."

Another bit of advise — if this or something similar, or something that goes bump in the night happens in a class, ask the teacher for assistance. The teacher cannot help if s/he isn't asked. Teacher assistance is included in the class registration fee.

CALLING IN OF GOD THE FATHER ALMIGHTY AND SHEKENAH, THE FEMININE ASPECT OF THE CREATOR: *God The Father Almighty, Teacher, Consoler, Warrior Who protects all that I have created! Come into my being, into my essence! Bring with You energies of wisdom, knowledge, communication, spark of life, spark of creation! Universal Energies of healing, magic, power, love, fatherly love! Lend me Your power, lend me Your might, bring Your magic and healing to my sight! I invoke Thee, I summon Thee, I call Thee forth! I invoke Thee, I summon Thee, I call Thee forth! I invoke Thee, I summon Thee, I call Thee forth! Come into my heart with the 4 winds, 4 directions, 4 seasons, 4 elements and Goddess.*

Shekenah, loving Mother from the Womb of Creation, Come into my being, into my essence! Bring with You energies of healing, love, mercy, grace, forgiveness, compassion, beauty & harmony, order & symmetry, Earth magic, Earth healing, Earth power, Earth love, motherly love! Lend me Your power, lend me Your might, bring Your magic and healing to my sight! I invoke Thee, I summon Thee, I call Thee forth! I invoke Thee, I summon Thee, I call Thee forth! I invoke Thee, I summon Thee, I call Thee forth! ! Come into my heart with the 4 winds, 4 directions, 4 seasons, 4 elements and God The Father Almighty.

EXERCISE: From your heart pray, "Teach me to love as You Love. Help me find the still point from which creation is possible. Help me to create my life in Divine Order and for the highest good of all concerned."

Be very still. Feel the request and love leaving the heart center. Let it go! Go deeper into the stillness behind the physical eyes. Allow the breath to slow and become shallow. If you need a point of concentration, focus on the breath entering and leaving through the nostrils. Or repeat a mantra, such as OM, either on every exhale, or say the mantra independent of the breath. Go deeply within until you are aware of your inner presence. You will come to what seems a precipice; step off and into Great Spirit.

EXERCISE: The same request might also be sent out with deep Yoga breathing.

CALLING IN OF THE GREAT STAR NATION AND THE GALACTIC CONFEDERATION: *I call upon the Great Star Nation and the Galactic Confederation.*

Once upon a time, a great civilization called Atlantis sank further and further south of the equator. When it reached the South Pole it became frozen under miles of ice. Because the Atlanteans misused spiritual forces, spiritual wisdom was broken up and given only in pieces to the various groups of humans who survived the catastrophe. No one group was given the whole package of spiritual wisdom. Native Americans were the only ones who were given the knowledge that life and humanity exist on other planets in the galaxy.

It is estimated that a quarter of the American population has seen some kind of spiritual apparition. It is also true that millions of individuals across the globe have seen spaceships. Within tubular, aluminum-like spaceships are skinny, large-headed beings in grey spacesuits, who are rumored to be responsible for abductions of citizenry. There are also beings, who look very much like us. These humans travel in saucer-like crafts that are propelled not by fossil, nuclear or even hydrogen fuel, but inter-dimensionally by an advanced technology. Their mandate might be compared to the fictional character, James Kirk, and the crew of the Starship Enterprise. For lack of a better word, they might be referred to as the Galactic Confederation.

Galileo looked out at our solar system and beyond with a telescope made in Holland. Galileo and his Dutch contemporary, Hoygans, predicted that there would be other planets similar to Earth and that humans would be found living on these worlds. Science in one respect is the study of Creation. Once a successful model is made, it is possible for the universe to independently repeat the model.

EXERCISE, WHICH MIGHT BE A GUIDED MEDITATION OR JOURNEY: Invite a member of the Galactic Confederation to come to you. Ask her/him to show you how they are helping Earth to go into the Golden Age of the Return of the Angels. Ask to be shown what the Golden Age of the Return of the Angels is all about.

EXAMPLE: From Reiki & Other Rays of Touch Healing:

One high drama is the story in the Old Testament of fallen angels luring mankind into the pits of hell. The good news is that God gave Lucifer and the third of the angels who fell with him only a short time to tempt man and their time is ending now! In all great past civilizations there existed a common prophesy, the coming of a great Golden Age, a thousand years of Light, love, peace, joy, illumination, fulfillment - The Golden Age of the Return of the Angels. If man so chooses, the time can be extended for another thousand years.

Aztec, Mayan, Egyptian and Incan 100,000-year calendars have all come to a close within the past 20 years. Even the Australian Aborigines' calendar came to an end in August 1987, the month and year of the harmonic convergence, when all of the planets lined up. The Piscean Age is over and quite literally "this is the dawning of *The Age of Aquarius.*" The song that was written over two decades ago is about to become a reality. Earth is in the process of changing roles; she is moving from serving as a repository for the working out of undesirable thought forms into a premier position in this universe. Another planet will serve as a kidney for this universe.

In December 2012, the calendar found within the I Ching drops into 'no time'. It is not just 'old people' who feel that time is on roller skates. I remember 3rd grade as being a lifetime unto itself; it's no longer that way for children. Einstein proved that time does not exist the way in which we perceive it. That in order to consider time, it must be relative to space. We are on the verge of entering a whole new world.

CALLING IN OF THE PLANT KINGDOM: *I call upon the plant kingdom and blessed herbs, flower essences, essential oils, nature spirits, dryads, gnomes, sylphs, salamanders and undine, elves, sprites, fairies, divas, over-lighting diva of healing, master divas of the flowers — rose, lilac, lily of the valley!*

EXERCISE, WHICH MAY BE DONE AS A JOURNEY OR IN MEDITATION: See yourself clearly in your mind's eye standing in a beautiful place in nature. Ask one of the nature spirits to take you to your favorite flower. Ask to become very small and explore the flower — stem, petals, scent and color.

INSTRUCTOR: We have already discussed how anything with DNA has a consciousness and that there are other universes and dimensions.

CALLING IN OF THE STONES: *I call upon the stone people, mineral, quartz, crystal and gem kingdoms! Gem, crystal, quartz elixirs! Power of the mountains and large stones!*

EXERCISE, WHICH MAY BE DONE AS A JOURNEY OR IN MEDITATION: See yourself clearly in your mind's eye standing in a beautiful place in nature. Ask one of the nature spirits to take you to a crystal. What kind of crystal are you standing in front of? Imagine that all of the cells in your body turn and face the side so that you become invisible. Walk into the crystal! Ask for the healing properties of the crystal to heal you.

EXERCISE: If the class is being held near a place in nature, everyone is invited to write down a question that s/he would like to know the answer to. Put the piece of paper in a pocket or purse. At lunchtime, go outside and look for a rock that appeals to you. Take out the piece of paper and reread the question. See if there is a figure or design on the rock that answers the question.

CALLING IN OF THE POWER ANIMALS: *I summon the winged — eagle, hawk, raven, crow, hummingbird, pheasant, owl, falcon!*
    I call upon the four-legged — horse, antelope, bear, beaver, otter, lynx, tiger, elephant, wolf, dog, fox, coyote, ram!
    I call forth the six-legged — grasshopper, cricket, dragonfly, butterfly, scarab, ant.
    I call upon the eight-legged — Mother Spider.
    I summon the finned — whale, dolphin, porpoise, shark, salmon, seahorse!
    I call the creepers and crawlers — lizard, snake, turtle, salamander, crocodile, alligator!

EXERCISE, WHICH MAY BE DONE AS A JOURNEY OR IN MEDITATION: See yourself clearly in your mind's eye standing in a beautiful place in nature. Ask for your power animal to come to you. Which one comes? What is her/his gift for you? Ask your power animal to take you on a journey so that you might become closer to nature and all of God's creatures.

EXAMPLE: To find out what gift an animal brings to humanity, look at its primary characteristic. The energies of seahorse are primordial. Because salmon travels the vast oceans and learns much before returning up the river to spawn, salmon represented wisdom to the Celts. With their large jaws and rows of extremely sharp teeth, crocodiles and alligators have the ability on another level to grab negativity and spin it upwards to the Light

57

for transformation. There is a book, Medicine Cards, by Sams & Carson that gives detailed explanations of other power animals. In addition, the animals might have special gifts for the one who seeks the aid of power animals.

CALLING UPON OTHER SPIRITUAL GROUPS: *I call upon the Holy Ghost and Holy Spirit! I call upon my twin flame, and my own I Am presence! I call upon my ancestors — those who have walked before me and those who are yet to come! All whom I have summoned, named and unnamed who come in the Love of Buddha and the Light of Christ, please be here and present now!*

The Church holds that the Holy Ghost and Holy Spirit are mystery elements. In fact, the Holy Ghost and Holy Spirit may be included among the 20-count above. Some spirits are more evolved than others; all have their distinct place in the Grand Scheme of Creation. Holy Spirit may also allude to the Great Spirit that permeates this universe.

EXERCISE: The Yin/Yang symbol reminds us that there is always a spot of masculine in the feminine, and a spot of feminine in the masculine. Females have 2/3 feminine and 1/3 masculine energy; males have 2/3 masculine and 1/3 feminine energy. We also have a counterpoint that holds the other 2/3 — 1/3 balance. This other aspect of ourselves may well be our guardian angel, who watches out for us from the world of spirit. In meditation feel the pink cord that connects you to your twin flame. Ask that you might see your twin flame.

First Task

The opening ceremony may be used to either bring something into fruition or to banish something. As has been previously stated, Shamanism works with the natural world. The moon is a powerful part of that world, and is more than just a beautiful luminary in the night sky. Without the moon life on Earth would be exceptionally harsh.

To incorporate the moon into ceremony, one must know where the moon is in its cycle. The full moon is a time for fulfillment, to reap the benefits of ones efforts. Magic that is decreasing in nature, such as losing a bad habit, disease, pain, debts, or extra pounds, is best begun after the full moon. This allows the waning moon to assist in diminishing the unwanted trait. When the moon is completely dark, it is a good time to plant a seed of thought. As the moon becomes larger, it is a good time to manifest. The waxing moon helps prayers, petitions or wishes to grow.

Depending upon where the moon is, workshop participants think of something that they would either like to bring into earth form, or banish from their lives. It is best that the intention be clear, but at the same time to be a general idea. In this way, the details are left to God. For example, if a new home is desired, simply ask for a home and wonder what God has in mind. In asking for money it is best to have a purpose in mind for the money, such as, a vacation, a new car, etc. If romance is desired, asking for a specific individual is manipulation of another's freewill choice. Frequently, our worst waking nightmares are situations we have manipulated into existence.

Yes, several requests may be made in the ceremony. However, this has a shotgun consequence; in other words, the energy, like buckshot, tends to scatter. Having one particular goal in mind has the effect of a bullet or arrow. It is not just by the spiritual energy the Shaman is channeling that increases the probability of a petition being answered. It is also the focused, concentrated attention of the participant, which brings about results.

It is much easier for first-time Shamanic workshop attendees if they have meditated previously. Some individuals have had the opportunity to see themselves in meditation during a healing session. If an individual does not have meditation experience, the Shaman conducting the class holds the energy in the circle so that all might experience the Otherworlds.

The next step is to set aside a place to honor Holy Spirit. The room or space is cleared and spiritual forces are called in. These topics were dealt with in the last chapter. For this particular ceremony, the 4 directions, 4 winds and 4 elements, as well as God and Goddess are not called in because they are involved in the ceremony. As God is personified in nature, in Native American Shamanism, Father Sky represents the masculine attributes of God; Mother Earth represents the feminine attributes of Goddess.

INSTRUCTOR: I will beat the drum seven different times. Rather than listening to the pounding, focus on the droning of the drum. Each time the drumming begins you will see yourself clearly in your mind's eye standing in a beautiful place in nature. For each of the directions a specific power animal will be suggested. The details of each direction are being explained now so that there is an overview of the ceremony; like reading the chapter titles before reading a book. Once the ceremony begins, the specific instructions for the upcoming direction will be repeated. After the drumming for each direction, there will be a short pause. It is important to remember that if another animal comes, it is best go with that power animal. It maybe that that particular bird or animal has the energy to help you manifest your desire! In each direction you may always ask the animal questions.

EXAMPLE: One man asked for self-esteem. Rather than hawk, rooster came to guide him. Who has more pride than rooster?

INSTRUCTION FOR GOING TO FATHER SKY: When I begin beating the drum you will see yourself clearly in your mind's eye standing in a beautiful place in nature. You will travel with hawk, the messenger, to Father Sky. With your heart you will carry and present your prayer or plea to Father Sky. *(Rapid, repetitive, non-varying drumbeat on the same place on the drum for 8 to 10 minutes.)*

INSTRUCTION FOR GOING TO THE EAST: When I begin beating the drum you will see yourself clearly in your mind's eye standing in a beautiful place in nature. You will travel with crow, who knows the mysteries of creation, to the East, the place of fire. You will cleanse your prayer

61

in the fire. Then you will step into the fire and cleanse yourself. Then you will become fire. You will feel what it is like to dance in the hot coals. Feel the power! Be fire! *(Rapid, repetitive, non-varying drumbeat on the same place on the drum 8 to 10 minutes.)*

INSTRUCTION FOR GOING TO THE SOUTH: When I begin beating the drum you will see yourself clearly in your mind's eye standing in a beautiful place in nature. You will travel with lynx, who is the keeper of lost magic, to the South, the place of water. You will cleanse your prayer in the water. Then you will step into the water and cleanse yourself. Then you will become water. You will feel what it is like to be translucent and liquid. Be water! *(Rapid, repetitive, non-varying drumbeat on the same place on the drum 8 to 10 minutes.)*

INSTRUCTION FOR GOING TO THE WEST: When I begin beating the drum you will see yourself clearly in your mind's eye standing in a beautiful place in nature. You will travel with lizard, who is the dreamer, to the West, the place of earth. You will cleanse your prayer in the earth. Then you will go into a rock, crystal or mud bath and cleanse yourself. Then you will become earth. You will feel what it is like to be solid yet vibrating with the electromagnetic energy of earth. Be earth! *(Rapid, repetitive, non-varying drumbeat on the same place on the drum 8 to 10 minutes.)*

INSTRUCTION FOR GOING TO THE NORTH: When I begin beating the drum you will see yourself clearly in your mind's eye standing in a beautiful place in nature. You will travel with white buffalo, who is wise, to the North, the place of air. You will cleanse your prayer in the wind. Then you will rise up on a puff of air and cleanse yourself. Then you will become air. You will feel what it is like to be transparent and free. Be air! *(Rapid, repetitive, non-varying drumbeat on the same place on the drum 8 to 10 minutes.)*

INSTRUCTION FOR GOING INTO MOTHER EARTH: When I begin beating the drum you will see yourself clearly in your mind's eye standing in a beautiful place in nature. You will find an opening into the Earth and travel with horse, who is power, to the cobalt blue heart of Mother Earth. The spirit of Earth is sometimes referred to as Hava, the mother of all living. You will ask Mother Earth or Hava to ground your prayer. *(Rapid, repetitive, non-varying drumbeat on the same place on the drum 8 to 10 minutes.)*

INSTRUCTION FOR THE SEVENTH DIRECTION: When I begin beating the drum you will see yourself clearly in your mind's eye lying down on your back in a beautiful place in nature. You will feel your heart center. Then you will connect your heart to the heartbeat of Mother Earth. There have been people who have done this and healed themselves. When you are through send a prayer of gratitude from your heart to all who have helped you on your journey. *(Slow, double beat for 8 to 10 minutes.)*

When everyone has returned from their inward journey, all are given an opportunity to share their experiences. Not sharing is always an option. The exercises within the ceremony help the teacher to know who is able to see themselves and who is having trouble. Some workshop participants are able to feel themselves in these Otherworlds but do not see themselves. For these particular individuals there is the bathroom exercise. That is, during the break or at lunch it is suggested that they go into the ladies' or men's room and look at themselves in a mirror for one whole minute. This will seem like a long time. Afterwards, they are to close their eyes and hold the image from the mirror in their mind's eye. If the image is lost, the advice is to look into the mirror again and repeat the exercise.

EXPERIENCES OF MARY K HAYDEN OF IRELAND: During the initiation into the Order of Melchizedek there was a feeling of energy going up and down my body. Then the soles of my feet burned, particularly the right one. The heat came up to my knees and there was an overall sense of wisdom. My journey into the directions was different.

From almost the beginning of the ceremony, my body was paralyzed, the same way it does when I get a healing. On my journey to Father Sky, one of my cats flew in the air with eagle and myself. As I was asking questions of Father Sky, my other 3 cats appeared. They told me that they were there to support me.

The East surprised me because fire is scary for me. With the smoke, I coughed and then thought, "OK I'm clearing something." The flame became a happy, fluid dance that I found freeing. I loved being the tall flame, and then changing in size and direction.

In the South I cleansed myself gently in the water because I am learning to swim late in life. I don't put my head under water; however, in order to become water, I had to. In doing so I found that I had released another fear. Then I became a small drop of water on a stone.

Bear came to me in the West. I loved bear! My power animals are typically cuddly. When I dove into the earth it was brown clay, like the Irish soil - clean and rough at the same time. I loved the connection. It was like I had tentacles from my hands and feet that went into the earth. When I became earth, I was helping seeds to grow. I felt really healthy and full of nutrients.

In the North I started off feeling a cool breeze and then I became the cool breeze. I would cool people. Then I became a bit naughty and turned warm.

I rode horse into the Earth quickly, and felt a strong connection with the Earth. I asked questions of Hava and received answers.

With the heart, I just opened my heart and invited the elements and directions in to heal my heart. There was both a great sense of comfort and extreme heat; also a sense of wholeness.

EXPERIENCE OF DORTHY OF NORTH CAROLINA, WHO DID NOT WISH TO HAVE HER REAL NAME USED: During the initiation into the Order of Melchizedek, I decided to surrender to the rhythm of the circling and let it happen. I tried to do the same thing on the journey — watch myself and see what happens.

Owl came and took me to Father Sky. As we flew together, owl tried to take a negative thought from me that I have been trying to release for a long time. Eventually, I let go and he took care of it. I felt very small next to owl.

In the East, as with all of the directions, a visual release of spiritual heaviness was followed by a release in my own body. While in the fire heaviness within me simply melted away.

Jaguar went with me to the South while coyote looked on. At the water Jaguar hesitated before going in. Once in the water, he helped the water to shoot through my solar plexus to release more heaviness.

I traveled on brown bear's stomach, not his back, to the West. That really surprised me! Then I became Alice in Wonderland. More heaviness dissipated as brown bear and I went into the earth.

White bear just materialized in the North. Then he became a cloud. The weight I have been carrying went into the cloud and then the cloud disappeared.

Horse started down with me into Mother Earth, but he didn't stay. Initially, I went down again as Alice in Wonderland. After horse disappeared, spider appeared, followed by a beautiful, mystical snake. Turtle appeared with the 12 astrological signs on his back. It was quite nice because we flew down together. Then I found myself as a crystal.

I called back all of the experiences I had had. I asked for healing for all of mankind and then for myself. I still feel the peace that doing that brought to me.

EXPERIENCE OF SUSAN HARRIS OF ENGLAND:
I became water in a lake. An animal drank

66

me. After going through the body of the animal, I came out as urine. It was not a dirty feeling at all — it was simply nature. I was a part of a cycle and I was experiencing it firsthand. Then I ran over stones and out to sea. In the process I was purified. After playing in the sea I was evaporated into a cloud. I came down as rain into a lake, and the process was repeated

EXPERIENCE OF HANNI BLOMBERG OF SWEDEN DURING THE CEREMONY: I saw an eagle. It was big! He turned, looked at me and said, "Take your seat and hang on!"

In the East I felt the fire and saw the color of fire all around me. In the South the water became a huge wave and then it had the image of a woman's face. I felt the earth in the West, and felt a release in the air. In the Earth, Hava touched my heart.

EXPERIENCE OF ANGELA JOHANSSON OF SWEDEN IN THE NORTH: When I went to the North I felt an old gunshot wound in my neck. It had to be from another lifetime. The injury healed during the journey. It feels good now, and my neck is very warm.

EXPERIENCE OF ANDREAS BLOMBERG OF SWEDEN DURING THE CEREMONY: On the way to Father Sky I saw three small eagles waiting for food from their parents. I realized it was a valley in the Alps that I had been to. The other memorable experience occurred in the East. I took the fire into my body. It felt hot, but not now!

EXPERIENCE OF TRUDY VAN DER JAGT OF THE NETHERLANDS: While you were beating the drum to clear the room, I went deep inside myself. I felt something come up, which I blew away.

I flew with seagull to Father Sky, and asked him why he was with me. He said, "You are always collecting white feathers for the angelic powers. Now I am here altogether."

The East was not so intense. The water in the South was nice — everything I wanted to let go of went out to the sea. Then I became water.

In the West I put the dirty stuff into a hole and buried it. Then I became the ground itself. In the North I became very hot and connected to the air.

I went with a black horse into Mother Earth, but my white horse came along as well. Hava greeted us. Hava was a thick, fat mama. She rode on my white horse and took my burdens.

EXPERIENCE OF DENISE OF THE NETHERLANDS IN THE CEREMONY: There was so much happening when you cleared the room. The direction that surprised me the most was the South. I had to go South with coyote but when we reached the water there were elephants. I became the water that shot out of their trunks. A couple of times on the journey I became Tinker Bell — that too was amazing. I loved the part about Mother Earth. I gave her everything!

EXPERIENCE OF PATRICIA ROSEBOOM OF THE NETHERLANDS IN THE CEREMONY: There is always a lot of chattering and noise in my head. I was able to shut it down during the clearing. The most interesting direction was Father Sky. I flew on the back of a big bird, but a smaller bird came and told me

68

that he was better. So, I went with him. I had difficulty seeing myself, but I let go of my garbage. It was interesting; I went with hippo to the water.

EXPERIENCE OF JOAO RAMOS OF PORTUGAL: I don't see all of the colors when I meditate. When you cleared the room, I started to see all of the colors. A strong white light came in front of my 3rd eye and then disappeared. But it kept coming back.

On the way to Father Sky I was in front of eagle, traveling backwards and looking into his eyes.

I had a strong pain in my shoulder. In the West I put it in the earth and the pain in my body left. It's still gone!

EXPERIENCES OF FRANK OF THE NETHERLANDS DURING THE CEREMONY: During the clearing I felt something in my spine going away. As you beat the drum so that we could travel to Father Sky, I saw a mosquito that turned into a bird. Then an owl came and told me to stay in my body. She said that the journey was inner work. I astral travel and the owl's message surprised me. In the East I walked on hot coals. In the South I went into a river with a hippo and crocodile.

EXPERIENCES OF VICKIE EBERLEIN OF GEORGIA: Yes, I saw myself in each of the directions. When I was fire, I was fire. I totally did not expect that. In the water I became the whitecaps and then a giant wave.

EXPERIENCES OF DONNIE HUNTER OF GEORGIA: The first time, I was met by porcupine! I love porcupine! Then vulture came! He had a long, long neck. I asked him why he had come. He told me that he cleans up death so that new things can grow. I reached Father Sky where everything was enveloped in white, beautiful light. A horse ran beside me when I went into Mother Earth. She took me to the top of a mountain and we looked out into a valley.

EXPERIENCES OF RYAN ALLEN NEAL OF FLORIDA: My highlights would be going into fire and feeling like fire. I was part of the burning intensity. I became water. It was all just there. The animal that kept coming to me was a barn owl — one of those large white owls. We flew around! When I went into Mother Earth there were a lot of colors.

EXPERIENCES OF DOMINIKA KULIGOWSKA OF POLAND: Going into fire was the most important part. I felt really connected to it. I became fire and I could touch things and they would catch on fire. It wasn't painful; it wasn't a destructive fire. It was like rebirthing.

EXPERIENCES OF ANTHONY TORRES OF GEORGIA: I saw myself envisioning the places that I was visioning going to. A force of light came into me. Before going into any of the directions, all of the animals that I traveled with would stare me directly in the eye, and give me a determined look of absoluteness.

In each of the directions, when it came time for me to present my petition, the parchment became laced in gold and encapsulated in ruby red. In the east I merged with the fire - that started a process of burning away the fears that were involved with me fulfilling my petition. I

70

allowed that to happen. I allowed the fears and doubts to burn. In the south I went with porcupine. When I reached the water I went into the water with a blue bird, a red bird and a turtle.

INSTRUCTOR: Just as God is much more than we could possibly comprehend, so too, our own soul is much too large to fit into any one human body. Just as we are both individuals and a part of the great circle of creation, so too, the personalities of our different incarnations are both unique and a part of our larger soul. In addition to this, each personality has different facets. So, it is possible in meditation or journeywork to watch ourselves in meditation watching yet another aspect of ourselves doing something else. What is the benefit of this? It helps us to have some understanding that we are multidimensional beings. It also helps us to get in touch with abilities from other lifetimes that would benefit us at certain times in our current lifetime.

As for surrounding your petition in gold, that helped protect it and raise its vibration. The ruby red helped to ground your wish.

VIOLET FLAME ATTUNEMENT: The energy of the Violet Flame is healing and manifestation through transformation. Transformation is used in healing when diseased tissue is turned into healthy tissue. Healing may occur in any number of different ways, which will be discussed throughout the book. An example of transformation magic happens when the Shaman likens something that has already occurred to something that s/he would like to come about. For example, jealousy might be looked at as a nudge from the individual's own higher self, telling her/him that it is time to bring something like what is being envied into the Shaman's life. It would be considered black magic to try to take something away from another person. However, to ask God for something similar to what the other person has maybe done. So, the Shaman might say, "Shekenah, God The Father Almighty, Christed Beings, Buddhas, elemental, angels, blessed ones, so as you brought a red Jaguar into Tom's garage, so to bring a new car into my garage."

Requests, like this one, may happen soon, or the petition may set a whole series of practical events into play. It may begin by going back to school to learn other skills. The best possible advice is to clearly state the petition and leave the details to God.

God would never ask anyone to do harm or kill another. Death is not a desirable solution to a problem; issues are to be worked out amongst the living. When an issue is not worked out, something similar keeps on occurring until the participants call a halt to the drama. At this point, they may stop to consider their role, how they are contributing and to change.

Anyone may work with the Angels of the Violet Fire or the Violet Flame. There is a difference in level of communication and aptitude before and after the attunement. To demonstrate the altering effect of the attunement, a meditation is given in two parts. In the first part of the meditation the students are asked to see themselves clearly in their minds eye. The Angels of the Violet Fire and the Violet Flame are invited in. The students work with the angels and the Violet Flame. Then they are guided to go with the Angels of the Violet Fire to three different locations. In each city or place they are asked to stand between two of the angels and ask what to do. Questions maybe asked of the angels, but the task at hand may or may not seem logical or make sense. After the first part of the meditation, the instructor initiates the group one at a time into the Violet Flame. Then the instructor continues with the second part of the meditation whereby the initiates are guided back to the same localities to work with the angels in the same manner. Afterwards, everyone is invited to share her/his experiences. As always, not sharing is an option.

INSTRUCTOR: The Violet Flame initiation is given at the crown (top of the head), back heart chakra and front heart chakra. The first two times I tap you on the shoulder put your hands in prayer position over your head. The third time I tap you on the shoulder put your hands in prayer position over your sternum.

EXPERIENCES OF MARY K HAYDEN OF IRELAND: In the meditation there was an immediate feeling of great peace and tranquility. I saw a lot of people that I had seen in the Upperworld step into the Violet Flame. There were other souls who were here for the course and very happy for the transformation.

When we went to Washington DC there were millions of Angels of the Violet Fire around. They asked me to surround and fill everything with love. We started with the White House — every inch. We went on to the Senate and lots of government buildings, and to send it to the politicians. The second time, the moment we got there the angels were bigger and there was stronger energy.

Ireland was very interesting. Archangel Raphael asked me to fill the country with emerald green healing light. The second time the emerald green was pulsating; the people and land were absorbing the energy. You could see the green healing being sucked down.

In Israel and Palestine the angels asked me to send pink love light to everyone, to the land and to the territorial nature of the people. When I went back the second time, I felt great sadness. There was some absorption of the healing, but it was like they were not ready for healing. The angels asked me to keep sending healing.

During the initiation into the Violet Flame I had a great sense of being humbled and great gratitude poured out from my heart. Immediately, when you stood in front of me, there appeared a great, strong dark purple energy — really strong. It stayed with me. The angel told me, "The initiation is to make you strong so more people can benefit."

EXPERIENCES OF DOROTHY OF NORTH CAROLINA, WHO DID NOT WANT HER NAME USED: Immediately, my mother came. It was provocative looking at her in the eye and loving her. Other women in my family with the same issues were grateful to be there. We sent violet energy like fireworks in every direction.

In Washington, DC, I went to the White House and started sprinkling positive thoughts. The second time, I went back to the White House to hold positive energy for the White House and mankind.

The first time in Ireland, I sprinkled positive thoughts, like pixy dust, on the elementals. The second time, they gave it back to me.

In Israel and Palestine I went to the Temple Wall and prayed, particularly for the people who were there at the time. It was powerful sitting there. The second time, I merged the energies of the metaphysical world into the body of Israel.

The Violet Flame attunement was prayerful! My hands stayed in prayer position after the initiation.

INSTRUCTOR: Rebuilding of the Temple of Solomon is not what people think it is. Rather than a physical structure, the scriptural meaning is the rebuilding of metaphysics and spiritualism.

EXPERIENCE OF TRUDY VAN DER JAGT OF THE NETHERLANDS: In Washington DC the angels told me, "We will take care of the politics, you do your job." The initiation felt solid.

INSTRUCTOR: Some people are not allowed to involve themselves in political situations. It may be a past life issue? In any case, you did the right thing by following the angels' suggestion.

EXPERIENCE OF DENISE OF THE NETHERLANDS: I worked with the angels to fix the dikes in New Orleans. Then we went to Holland and did the same thing.

EXPERIENCE OF PATRICIA ROSEBOOM OF THE NETHERLANDS: I received pretty much the same message as my sister in Washington DC. The angels said, "Stick to your own thing. It's OK! It will get better!"

During the attunement the energy went down my spine when you lifted my head.

EXPERIENCE OF JOAO RAMOS OF PORTUGAL: I felt heavier before the initiation. During the attunement I saw colors. Your hands on my shoulders were light.

EXPERIENCES OF FRANK OF THE NETHERLANDS: I saw a lot of violet.

EXPERIENCES OF VICKIE EBERLEIN OF GEORGIA: In stepping into the Violet Flame, I felt my body becoming the Violet Flame and I could see the flickering of the fire. During the meditation, the first time we went to Washington DC, I was asked to send healing to the buildings — the White House, senate, and congress, and to clear out stagnant energy and replace that with understanding, compassion and unconditional love. When we went to Louisiana, I was asked to spread crystals all over the land — they were sparkling blue, purple and pink. When we went to New York City, I was asked to do a healing with the Egyptian Cartouche symbol, the LOTUS, on Ground Zero.

The second time we went to Washington DC, I was asked to put some disks into a reflective pool. When I asked why, I was told that it was to change the vibration of the water; by changing the vibration of the water it would change the vibration of the surrounding areas as the water goes through everything. The second time we went to

76

Louisiana, I was given a bucket of marbles and flower petals. I was asked to roll the marbles down the city streets. When I did this, they went into the land to begin healing the land. Then I went up and was asked to strew flower petals all over the land and into the water.

EXPERIENCES OF DONNIE HUNTER OF GEORGIA: During the initiation I saw one giant violet flame. I saw an angel, named Quasi, and myself standing in front of a mirror. There were hands on my shoulders and back. The first time we went to Louisiana, a light came, like the light of a car headlight, and we worked it back and forth over the state. The second time, a maroon ribbon was woven into the land. In New York at Ground Zero I saw a huge circle of angels and spirits.

EXPERIENCES OF RYAN ALLEN NEAL OF FLORIDA: I saw the Flame and the energy upwards. In Washington DC I felt more like being involved in politics, working against corruption and greed, and influencing politicians to be open to the world and not so demanding upon the world. In Louisiana I am giving my time, energy and contributions to put a fresh face on the land.

EXPERIENCES OF DOMINIKA KULIGOWSKA OF POLAND: During the initiation I could feel the Violet Flame on my face, especially on my cheeks, and heat in my palms. It was a strong vibration! Very strong! When I was asked to help the angels, I was asked to do the same things. The first time it was on a smaller scale. In Washington DC I was asked to heal the thoughts of politicians. The first time in Washington DC, I worked on one person. When we went back the second time after the initiation, I was able to work on more people and I could feel the energy spreading. In New York City I was asked to use pink light coming from my heart to heal other hearts and help people to be calmer and more loving. The second time, the pink light was stronger and I saw more people. In Louisiana I had a big vacuum cleaner. I was asked to remove the viruses and bacteria. The second time I saw people and their negative, sad thoughts and was able to remove them with the vacuum cleaner.

INSTRUCTOR: As you practice journeying you will develop more and more your sensations of touching, feeling, seeing and hearing.

EXPERIENCES OF ANTHONY TORRES OF GEORGIA: During the initiation I felt warmth through my body, especially my hands. I envisioned Quan Yen and Saint Germain. I stepped into a spiraling tunnel of violet light that reached as far as I could see. I could feel hands on my shoulders and back. Quan Yen put her purple hands and arms into my stomach. While we sat there I asked her what the difference was between working with the angels of the violet fire before and after the initiations.

The first time in Washington DC, I was not asked to do anything. In New York I was asked to send light and stillness to the collective consciousness of the people of New York City. When I went to Louisiana I was asked to help a representative of old men and a young child. The old black man, who was unshaven and wore an old, tattered hat. What was being healed in the elderly was a feeling of despair and an inability to progress in their lives. I was told that when children go through disasters, there is so much unknown in their minds that they lack the ability to formulate emotions concerning the situation because it is so out of their hands and so chaotic. It may create a mindset that locks children into a disaster-drawing mindset.

I was told to send thoughts of liberation and absolute reality to Washington DC. The change of perception of the decision-makers will ultimately come down the chain of command and affect everyone. I don't remember going back to New York the second time. The second time in Louisiana, I was asked to send healing to the water because it is very toxic.

INSTRUCTOR: When you come across something completely unexpected, something that you know that your conscious mind could not make up, you know that the Otherworlds are a reality. When you experience the results of working in the Otherworlds in this reality, you have more confidence. You have a place to go where dreams might become reality.

Every time you heal even the tiniest aspect within yourself, you are helping to heal the planet. Sometimes, issues are not minuscule. Whenever we judge someone harshly, that issue is within us. For example, Hitler was part Jewish, J. Edgar Hover was homosexual, and Harry Potter's Voldemort is half human/half magician.

More about the Otherworlds from Anne's grandmother from Between Two Worlds:

"To get from this world to the world of spirit, the traveler has to pass through a veil. As trees are the perfect connection between heaven and earth, trees also provide a vehicle with which to transcend the veil. While a companion beat the drum, Kevin saw himself in his mind's eye traveling into a hole in the trunk of the World Tree. The World Tree is an Oak whose roots descend into the Lowerworld and whose branches reach into the Upperworld. In the Lowerworld where the roots end, there are two wells - the Well of Forgetfulness is to the left, the Well of Remembrance is to the right."

Anne questioned, "What possible use is a Well of Forgetfulness?"

Grandmother continued, "In the branches of the World Tree are souls waiting to be reborn. They drink from the Well of Forgetfulness before they are born so that they might focus on the life they will be born into."

"What is found in the Well of Remembrance?"

"All knowledge and everything that has ever happened may be accessed in the Otherworlds. So, if the traveler were journeying to retrieve knowledge or look into the future, he or she would drink from the Well of Remembrance. The story of Fionn mac Cumhail and the Salmon from the well is really a story of the Well of Remembrance that is told commonly as a fairy tale. Only when an individual is ready to go on does a teacher, possessed of arcane wisdom, appear to instruct on Spiritual matters."

80

Power Animals and Nature Spirits

The Shaman's Underworld stands in stark contrast to the brimstone and fire underworld described in horrific detail in Christian literature. The torturous Christian underworld came into being in the Dark Ages in Europe. Since then, the term underworld has come to mean a hellish eternal demise for lost souls. Thus, when a Hollywood screenwriter hears that Anubis, the Egyptian jackal-headed hunting dog, is the guardian of the underworld, s/he assumes that Anubis is the personification of evil. Actually, the Egyptian underworld was where souls of the departed traveled to on the River Styx. Anubis has the power to safely cross all undesirable regions, in this as well as the unseen world. In the afterlife, Anubis protected souls on their journey to 'heaven' from darker forces. Anubis, the guardian, opened the way for the dead to reach Osiris and the Halls of Judgment.

The Shaman's Underworld is not 'heaven', though souls of the departed may travel there. It is a vast, beautiful place in nature filled with diverse settings and infinite possibilities. The Shaman's Underworld is the realm of the power animals, dryads (spirits of the trees), elementals, fairies and other nature spirits. Within this realm may be found places of healing, which include mud baths, crystal beds, bubbling waterfalls and much, much more. It is the place the Shaman journeys to when seeking answers, foretelling the future, creative inspiration or healing.

The Shaman makes this inner journey by focusing on an image of her/himself. In meditation the Shaman watches her/himself and observes the action. The intention of the journey is determined before setting out.

Covert branches of the government use psychics to find secret information. These psychics use a form of meditation called remote viewing, whereby the psychic deliberately changes the scene every few seconds. It is reasoned that in doing so, the psychic does not have time to alter the visuals received in the inner eye. The problem is that by the very act of intentionally changing the scene, they are manipulating what is received. They cut themselves short in that information does not always come immediately. Thus, they may not be giving themselves enough time to focus and get the answers. For example, a visual may come up and the psychic asks what it is. Ten seconds later, something else comes into the scene or a verbal message is given. The remote viewer misses all this because s/he has already moved on to the next scene.

INSTRUCTOR: During the twenty minutes that the drum is beaten, you may sit or lay down. If you choose to put a blindfold over your eyes, it will help to darken the theatre of your inner eye so that you will be able to see more clearly. I will use the same Shamanic drumbeat we used for the opening ceremony. This drumbeat will be used for all of the Journeywork we do.

When I begin beating the drum, you will see yourself clearly in your mind's eye standing in a beautiful place in nature. You will find an opening into the Underworld and travel through it. Traditionally, Shaman often traveled down a slanted tunnel. The Celts went into the World Tree and traveled down through the roots of the tree to the Underworld. We live in modern times! Some people take the elevator or escalator down. One individual even took a hot air balloon down. The rules that apply to this world are not necessarily applicable to the Otherworlds.

You will come out in a beautiful place in nature. Ask for your power animal to come and assist you on your journey. The intention of your journey is to explore the Underworld and find the places of healing. You get to ask questions! When I change the beat of the drum, it is time to come back. If you are in the middle of something please finish what you are doing and then come back. You will return the same way you went down.

EXPERIENCES OF MARY K HAYDEN OF IRELAND: Well, I found an old, old oak tree. I went into a knot and down through the roots. I came out into a Garden of Eden. A big brown bear, a wolf, grasshoppers and spiders greeted me. A fairy was sitting on the petal of a blue flower. She invited me to join her. I became small and sat with her. We slid into the center of the flower, down the stalk and into a crystal healing room. I saw every color under the sun. Animals and people were there to be healed. It was fascinating, they all took on the color of the crystal that they sat or laid upon.

When we left, the fairy took me back up the flower stem. I asked the wolf to take me to a place of healing. We walked through woodlands and into an opening where there were millions of beautiful bluebell flowers. I laid on them to be healed. Of course, I flattened them, but when I got up they straightened. I didn't want to leave any of these places.

The wolf walked me back to the brown bear, who took me to a cave. He showed me people and animals who did not want healing. The energy in this cave was dead flat. I felt it! These people and animals were kind of lost, and did not want to know about spirituality. They were dull and without joy. I asked bear why he'd taken me there. He answered, "You have to see both sides."

Bear took me to an edge where I stepped off into a cloud. There was a group of Native Americans sending healing to Mother Earth. There was a totem pole and a huge amount going on. They said that there are not enough people who look up or within.

EXPERIENCE OF DOROTHY OF NORTH CAROLINA, WHO DID NOT WISH TO HAVE HER REAL NAME USED: I went down as I always do — sliding downwards into a rainforest. The owl and elementals greeted me. I took a vine and swung into an illuminated tunnel. I ended up in a healing room. Cloth materialized and I wrapped it around me — all over. The fabric was embroidered with rainbow colors. Then the material became an effervescent, translucent healing energy.

Catapulting out of the tunnel through an opening, I was confronted with a dark, red and black face. I was afraid for a moment. I realized it was a mask and walked through it. The mask disappeared.

Then I went back through the tunnel to the healing room, where I found myself moving through a tunnel in the earth and into the universe. Then I went back through the tunnel to the healing room. Somewhere along the journey, the tunnel became like a metamorphic experience. I went from being a caterpillar to a butterfly to a fairy. The three stages seemed to happen simultaneously.

EXPERIENCE OF TRUDY VAN DER JAGT OF THE NETHERLANDS: I saw myself! I went into a cave and became a cavewoman. I went down and came out into a huge cave with diamonds. I left the cave through an entrance and saw a pond. I called for a power animal. Swan and boar came. Swan stepped into the water and invited me to ride upon her back while she swam. We went under a waterfall where I was cleansed. Afterwards, I lay on her back, drying off in her soft feathers under the warm sun. After a while, swan took me back to shore. Boar was waiting for me. He showed me some very red stones, which grounded me. Then I came back.

EXPERIENCES OF PATRICIA ROSEBOOM OF THE NETHERLANDS: I focused on myself. I went down in an elevator. When I stepped out of the elevator, someone came and put me into a CT scan. Then she put me in a shower with roses, lavender and Ylang Ylang. Afterwards, we went outside. I was guided into beautiful beds of flowers —

85

roses, lavender, and others. Someone else came to me. I asked for a power animal. A wolf, owl and hippo came.

EXPERIENCE OF JOAO RAMOS OF PORTUGAL: I was looking everywhere for a power animal when suddenly dog and eagle came to me. Next, I unexpectedly found myself riding on the back of an elephant. The landscape was very green. Then I saw myself next to a female relative's father, who died two years ago. He has not gone on; he possesses his daughter! I put my hands on her. I saw myself pushing him. He left!

EXPEIENCES OF FRANK OF THE NETHERLANDS: I went down a vortex of just light. A diamond shape and two Jesus-like figures met me.

EXPERIENCES OF VICKIE EBERLEIN OF GEORGIA: I went down into the Underworld in an Alice-in-Wonderland-type tunnel — the rabbit hole that she dropped into. All of the images I saw were a combination of Alice in Wonderland and Brian Froud-type beings. Little animals came out of the earth and helped me down. When I got down there, there was a woman on a cliff or ledge. She was a Native American woman and she was wearing a long cloak. She brought her arms out to the side; her arms turned into wings and she became a large, brown bird. I held onto her and we went flying around in loops.

One of the places we went to was Alaska. There were huge mountains and everything was lush and green. I looked down and could see bears coming out of the lakes. We also flew to Aztec or Mayan panoramas with different types of mountains and pyramids. There was a lot of gold and the pyramids were gold.

We came to other images. One of the lessons that I came to learn was freedom and trust. As I was seeing things I was trying to logically categorize them so that I could describe them later. Then I was told that I was being too logical. At that point, I started seeing things that I could not explain. The pictures were very different.

INSTRUCTOR: Your guides are quick, or they understand you too well. The consolation is that you are not alone! It is difficult for dominant, left-brained, logical people to let go in the Otherworlds and simply watch themselves interacting without trying to figure things out, or make things happen. Dominant left-brained people like to put a logical twist to illogical events and the mythical figures that they are seeing.

When you are able to quiet the logical mind, the creative mind is freed. Just think of some of the things that both you and other students in the class have seen. You could not have made these things up with your left brain. The other thing that happens when you let go of your left brain in the Otherworlds is that you begin to develop psychic abilities.

It's not that your left brain is completely out of the picture in the Otherworlds; without your left brain you would not be able to apply the information that comes to you from the Otherworlds. The opposite is true when you are adding a sum of figures; in mathematics your left brain predominates. However, the numbers you are adding are represented as symbols. Symbols are the language of the right brain.

EXPERIENCES OF DONNIE HUNTER OF GEORGIA: The first thing I saw were two golden lights. They were shaped something like two Hershey kisses on their sides and touching each other at the narrowest point. Then I went to a circle of healers. There were many angels and spirits. There was a table in the middle of the circle. I went into the circle and with me were the things that I have asked for. I asked, "Would I be a healer?"

"Yes!"

"Would I heal myself?"

"Yes!"

"Would I be able to reach the goals that I have set for myself?"

"Yes!"

The next place I went to was a large, cafeteria-type room. In the back there were windows after windows, and a huge arch. There was one golden figure sitting at a table. I joined him at the table.

INSTRUCTOR: We all have guides (angels, spirits and power animals) that travel with us all of the time. We are never alone. Some of these souls go through different lessons with us; some help us on our earth journey. Most do both! There are other angels, spirits and power animals that do not travel with us all of the time but come in when we are healing others or ourselves. Typically, whenever anyone does healing work for Mother Earth, legions of angels and spirit helpers are there to lend a hand.

DONNIE HUNTER: Why was my trip to the Underworld very quick?

INSTRUCTOR: You received what you needed and came back. It is not always necessary to stay in the Underworld for the full 20 minutes of the drumming. Other times, you may find yourself lingering in the Otherworlds when the drumming has stopped.

EXPERIENCES OF RYAN ALLEN NEAL OF FLORIDA: I stood in my field, if you will. All of these colors came down around me and turned into a drill, and I created my own way into the Underworld. I felt like I was going through a wormhole. I splashed down into a sea of colors and stayed in there for a while. Then I went into the wormhole again and came out to a place where there were people dressed like Tibetan monks. In the middle of the room was a hand-like machine, which had an orb. Within the orb was a universe. Everyone was planning, and I was a part of this group. The wormhole appeared and I went back to the sea of colors. Angels passed by and faces came out of nowhere. Suddenly, a Native American appeared and started dancing to the beat of the drum.

EXPERIENCES OF DOMINIKA KULIGOWSKA OF POLAND: I went down to the Underworld using an elevator. As soon as the doors opened I saw a huge red rose. There was a smaller bee next to it. I asked her to show me the places of healing. In time, the bee disappeared and I saw a big white bear. He looked at me and he wanted me to follow him. So, I followed him.

I spent the whole time in a great forest. It was pretty and it had a green light in it. Bear then showed me a fire and I saw many faces in that fire. Then I saw a small pond, also with faces. I went into the pond and merged with the water. I saw many creatures around me. They were probably fairies or maybe angels — I am not sure. Then I asked, "What am I doing here? What do I need now?"

I found myself in the forest again. I saw a huge ball of golden, liquid light. I didn't walk there, but I suddenly found myself in the ball. I felt peace. I stayed there until the end.

EXPERIENCES OF ANTHONY TORRES OF GEORGIA: I started from the same setting as my journeywork earlier. I was going about finding the passageway to the Underworld. I was in lush woods. Ahead of me to the right I found an ethereal box on the ground. I realized that this was the place where I was to begin my travel. I was able to clear away the grass and the earth. I went down and found myself climbing through a tree. I ended up coming out of one of its branches. When I touched the ground and looked back at the tree, I realized that there was no way that I could comprehend the networking of the branches.

I looked around and found that I was in the desert. I started walking. A red, black and white snake came towards me. He greeted me kindly and lovingly. I recognized the snake. He was on my right. Then a blond, albino snake appeared on my left. They guided me to a green, beautiful place and then to a flower. It was almost like a huge, cartoonish-like Venus flytrap. It was chest high and in the shape of a blossom. I could see the waves of pinkish-purple color. I noticed at the end of the flower that the violet energy of the flower sparkled off. I sat in lotus position meditating in front of the flower. The red snake crawled up next to my right side and the albino snake to my left. The flower had a poetic movement to it. It enveloped me and took me up, but my body was still there in front of the flower meditating with the snakes. My essence was a clear light form, and I became aware of myself in the flower. The flower was resonant. It told me that dysfunction perpetuates dysfunction. Anger perpetuates anger. Dysfunction and anger are seemingly inescapable until you get to the core from which dysfunction and anger come from. I was spinning, spinning, spinning — the speed was beyond comprehension. It spit me out and I became random particles. I recollected and went back into the flower.

The flower spit me out again and I walked to a lake, while my shell was still in meditation. My two former girlfriends are both water signs and very loving people. One has beautiful red hair and beautiful blue eyes. She was there and like a mermaid — the bottom half of her was fish-like and the top half a woman. She gave me a deep stare. My other ex-girlfriend, who is also a wonderful person, was also there and she was also a mermaid.

I was watching them swim with much fluidity, power, and grace. Then they came out of the water, but they were in woman-form. They both had this tribal energy about them; their hair and makeup were wild. The next thing I knew, all of the important women in my life appeared and sat in a circle. I was in the middle of the circle. My mother stood on the outside watching. All of the women in the circle started sending me mothering, nurturing energy. The energy lifted me off the ground. I felt it in my heart.

91

The next thing I knew, I re-entered the flower and then went into my physical body. I am watching the fluid, purple flower and then suddenly it went erect and started spinning. A being appeared; it was Saint Germain. He said, "I am the Violet Flame in person."

There was purple light coming from him. I sat there in meditation. Then I stood up and bowed. At the end the red snake coiled up my right arm and the blond snake coiled up my left arm.

In the Shamanic II class the students are asked to go into the Underworld as the Celts journeyed.

INSTRUCTOR: When I begin beating the drum you will see yourself clearly in your mind's eye standing in a beautiful place in nature. Look for the World Tree and find an opening. Go into the aperture and travel down the roots of the Tree. You will come out in a beautiful place in nature.

EXPERIENCE OF LENA LIDMALM OF SWEDEN: I came out in a very old forest with old trees; blue birds flew about. Brown bear came towards me. I asked him how to heal the pain in my back. He told me to get on his back. He took me to a waterfall and told me to stand under it. The weight of the water hurt initially, and then the cold water made it feel better. When I came out of the water, he laid down. I lay down next to him with my back against his belly, listening to the vibration of the drum. It touched my heart. When bear took me back to the tree, I heard a large cat purring. The sound was big and deep.

EXPERIENCE OF ANGELA JOHANSSON OF SWEDEN: I also came out into a very old forest of oaks. A large black cat approached me and we went into the earth. I could see nothing! Then I met a very old woman. She said that I must take care of my eyes. She placed her hands first on my eyes and then on my solar plexus. It was a strange feeling. I also felt the drumbeat in my heart and in my body.

EXPERIENCE OF ANDREAS BLOMBERG OF SWEDEN: It happened that I found a very large tree. I entered the tree, traveled down the roots and came out into a savanna. A snake of extraordinary size approached me. I was afraid and he went away.

INSTRUCTOR: It is natural to be afraid of things that we avoid on the physical plane. However, the laws governing the Otherworlds are different from Earth's physical laws. The next time this great snake appears you may try asking him why he has come and hear him out. The fact that he honored your fear and left is a good sign. You might also test the snake by invoking the power of the Christ by saying, "If you have come in the Light of Christ please stay; otherwise go away!"

EXPERIENCE OF HANNI BLOMBERG OF SWEDEN: I saw myself walking to the cherry tree in my backyard. I went into the tree and down the roots. I was surprised to find my grandmother waiting for me. I was 10-years old when she died. I loved her very much. I cried when I saw her. I told her that I had a weight in my heart. She told me, "Do not be afraid. Be yourself."

I cried almost the entire time I was with her. Before I left she told me, "You can always come back to see me."

INSTRUCTOR: Typically, spirits of the departed are found in the Upperworlds and animal spirits in the Lowerworlds. However, this is not a steadfast rule, as you have discovered for yourself.

EXPERIENCE OF WILLEM BOEREN OF THE NETHERLANDS: I found a hole in the World Tree. I walked down the roots and came out into a beautiful place, but clouds filled the sky. Melchizedek was on top of a mountain serving everyone and everything. A white, gray-black eagle met me. For the first time, a wolf met me. Merlin came to assist with my healing. Fish gave me wisdom. Wolf, to my surprise, gave me a rabbit for my sustenance. When I was healed, Merlin became brighter. Then I went into the elements to cleanse. Afterwards, I was able to fly with eagle. At the end, the clouds lifted. There was a blue sky with a golden sun.

INSTRUCTOR: It may be that the Merlin you saw was not the mythical Merlin but your own connection to magic or your magical body. Wolf is the teacher. By teaching others, your connection to magic and the healing arts will grow stronger.

EXPERIENCE OF MARIAN VALKENBURGH OF THE NETHERLANDS: I saw a hedgehog, elephant and eagle. I was flying! Then I saw a rope that took me to the beginning where a man beat me. This is the source of the hatred I feel in this lifetime. I came back to hedgehog, elephant and eagle and cut the rope. I was filled with love. Then I felt many hands healing me.

I know now that it doesn't matter what someone does; I can love!

INSTRUCTOR: We all have issues. Your willingness to share your struggles and conquests help others in the group.

EXPERIENCE OF JOAO RAMOS OF PORTUGAL: I went to a mountain where I climbed up to a village. But then I saw myself walking in a street in Holland.

I then went to a cave and was shown a glass case holding the Holy Grail. It was strange! The way I had taken to the Grail led me away. The path was like a labyrinth.

In the end I was an eagle flying. I could see the village from the air.

EXPERIENCE OF ANDRE BEUKERS OF THE NETHERLANDS: I came to the World Tree and I became a big tree whose roots surrounded Mother Earth. So, I went into the World Tree and traveled to the Underworld as a tree. I came out and changed into a Native American Shaman. I wore a wolf headdress with eagle feathers.

I came to a love bug, who gave me a shovel. We went back in time, when the Earth was a fireball. Spirit took the shovel. I was put into the fire where I burned away fear. We traveled again through time to when the rains came. Spirit put me in the rain and I was cooled down. Then I went into a hurricane to clear. At last, the shovel was returned to me, and I put the tree back into the ground. I came back as a human.

YOD: To help the workshop participants open their 3rd eye, the YOD attunement is administered. It is drawn over the crown chakra and blown into the heart center. This initiation opens psychic channels and helps the initiated to go beyond the astral body for knowledge. For example, psychics often read the mental projections — be they hopes or fears — that are within the energy field of an individual. Hopes and fears may be transitory and fail to come to fruition. In the Otherworlds the YOD attunement helps the traveling Shaman to perceive information that is outside the human energy field.

Oftentimes, workshop attendees feel a subtle vibration around the top of the head before the initiation is actually given. After the initiation there is a fine stream of energy that comes from the top of the head and into the center of the brain. To receive impressions from spirit, it is important that the noisy chattering in the brain cease.

The YOD attunement is the first initiation into the archetypal energies of the Egyptian Cartouche. In some cases Egyptian symbols represent ancient gods and goddesses, who personify helpful qualities. In other cases ancient gods and goddesses were once highly evolved souls who walked the earth in human form. Thoth may well have been a great healer in Atlantis. After his death, people found that they could call upon him and ask for healing, in much the same way many Christians ask Saint Lucy to heal the eyes, Saint Christopher to keep a traveler safe, and Saint Anthony, also called simply Tony by some of my Jewish

96

friends, to find lost articles. In the case of Thoth, Isis, etc., their names became synonymous with their strongest attributes.

Egyptians also developed symbols, which embodied abstract principles and elemental forces found in the Universe. These symbols were carefully designed using a kind of golden rule principle. Murray Hope has a book and set of cards called <u>The Way of the Cartouche</u> that explains the thought constructs behind these images.

To prepare the class for the initiation, the instructor guides the class in an Egyptian-orientated meditation. The meditator focuses on an image of her/himself during the meditation. Thus, the students get practice in seeing themselves in their mind's eye without the benefit of the drum. The instructor speaks slowly, pauses deliberately and continues in almost a monotone. What follows is the full meditation:

INSTRUCTOR: Take a deep breath, relax, exhale and go deeply within. Go deeply, deeply, deeply within to your own seat of consciousness, your own guru. Be with your breath. With every breath that you take, every beat of your heart go deeper, deeper, deeper within. Feel your body relaxing. If thoughts come in see them bubble up and out like so many Champagne bubbles and be with your breath. With every breath that you take, every beat of your heart, go deeper and deeper, deeper and deeper within. The sound of my voice takes you deeper. Even outside noises only serve to take you deeper and deeper, deeper and deeper.

See yourself clearly in your mind's eye standing in ancient Egypt. The landscape is green and lush. Cyprus trees are growing all about. Look at the monuments. They are covered in white stone and gilded in gold. They are enormous. Built very large so humans might keep themselves in perspective with the greater cosmos. Feel what it is like to stand in ancient Egypt. Touch something nearby. What is the texture? What is the temperature? Take a deep breath and smell the air.

Now begin walking. Feel your feet touching the ground as you walk on and on, on and on. Feel your legs carrying you forward from the hips, going deeper and deeper, deeper and deeper into the consciousness of ancient Egypt. A priestess joins you at your left side. Stop, turn and face her. Ask her, "What is your name?" Ask her, "What is your purpose?" Ask her any other questions you so wish.

And begin walking with the priestess at your left side. Feel your feet touching the ground as you walk on and on, on and on. Feel your legs carrying you forward from the hips, going deeper and deeper, deeper and deeper into the consciousness of ancient Egypt. A priest joins you at your left side. Stop, turn and face him. Ask him, "What is your name?" Ask him, "What is your purpose?" Ask him any other questions you so wish.

And begin walking with the priestess at your left side and the priest at your right side. Feel your feet touching the ground as you walk on and on, on and on. Feel your legs carrying you forward from the hips, going deeper and deeper, deeper and deeper into the consciousness of ancient Egypt. You come to the Sphinx. It is one large carved stone. As you stand facing the Sphinx, the left shoulder collapses, revealing a doorway. Open the door and look in. There are two passageways — one to the left and one to the right. Use your intuition to choose which passageway to take.

Step into the passageway with the priestess and the priest. Feel the ground beneath your feet. Touch the walls. What is this passageway like? Continue walking. Feel your feet touching the ground as you walk on and on, on and on. Feel your legs carrying you forward from the hips, going deeper and deeper, deeper and deeper into the consciousness of ancient Egypt. You come to large statue. With the priestess on your left side and the priest on your right stop, turn and face the statue. It is Thoth. In your mind's eye tell Thoth the password. He bids you go forth.

Thank Thoth and begin walking with the priestess at your left side and the priest at your right side. Feel your feet touching the ground as you walk on and on, on and on. Feel your legs carrying you forward from the hips, going deeper and deeper, deeper and deeper into the consciousness of ancient Egypt. You've come to a silver chalice. With the priestess on your left side and the priest on your right, stop and face the chalice. The chalice belongs to Nephthys. She asks you, "Why have you come?"

Tell her what you seek. She bids you, "Safe journey!"

Thank Nephthys, and begin walking with the priestess at your left side and the priest at your right side. Feel your feet touching the ground as you walk on and on, on and on. Feel your legs carrying you forward from the hips, going deeper and deeper, deeper and deeper into the consciousness of ancient Egypt. You've come to the hall of the animals. Sphinx is the guardian of the animal kingdom and the secret of animal medicine. There are many higher beings and angels here sending healing to the animal kingdom and the wilderness that is their home. With the priestess and the priest send healing energy to the animals and the wilderness. Send healing energy to the domestic animals and to their homes. See and feel healing going to the animals.

Now look for the exit, the door leading out. Walk to the exit with the priestess on your left side and the priest on your right. Open the door and look in. There is one single passageway. How is this passageway different from the last? Step into the passageway with the priestess and the priest.

Walk on with the priestess at your left side and the priest at your right side. Feel your feet touching the ground as you walk on and on, on and on. Feel your legs carrying you forward from the hips, going deeper and deeper, deeper and deeper into the consciousness of ancient Egypt.

You've come to a stone staircase. The steps are high and narrow. Begin climbing up the stairs with the priestess on your left side and the priest on your right. They are here to help you. Feel the strain in your upper legs as you climb up and up, up and up. Feel the sweat on your brow as you climb higher and higher, higher and higher.

You've come to a platform. With the priestess on your left side and the priest on your right turn and face the doorway. Open it. Look in. You are at the Queen's Chamber of the Great Pyramid. Step in. Isis, magician and healer, greets you. She escorts you to a crystal-healing table. She bids you lie down. Lie down upon the crystal-healing table. Higher beings and angels are here to assist you in your healing. Your body is rubbed with healing, scented oils. Take a deep breath and smell. Gemstones are placed on your body. Be on Isis' crystal-healing table in silence for one minute.

Know that you may return to the crystal-healing table at any time you so wish. Thank the higher being, angels and Isis for having assisted you in your healing process. Get off of the crystal-healing table and walk to the doorway with the priestess on your left side and priest on your right. Step through the doorway and out onto the platform.

Look up! There is another stone staircase. These steps too are high and narrow. Begin climbing up the stairs with the priestess on your left side and the priest on your right. They are here to help you. Feel the strain in your upper legs as you climb up and up, up and up. Feel the sweat on your brow as you climb higher and higher, higher and higher. You've come to a platform. With the priestess on your left side and the priest on your right turn and face the doorway. Open it. Look in. You are at the King's Chamber of the great pyramid. Step in!

Osiris, the great protector, greets you. He bids you to sit down upon a chair of light. You find that it magically supports you. Look around the room. It is a pyramid of rainbow light. Above you, the great moonstone capstone of the great pyramid draws healing energy to the Earth. Osiris calls upon the energy of Lotus, peace of mind. He touches your heart. Your heart opens like a thousand pedaled Lotus. See this clearly. Feel it. Osiris asks you to invoke your own higher self. Do this now. See the teacher that is you rise up out of your heart center, through the center of your body, through the middle of your head, up and out your crown. Your higher consciousness sits above your head. Ask your higher self to guide you through the day.

Osiris tells you that it is time for the initiation. He calls out and invokes God The Father Almighty and Sekhemet, The Goddess.

The teacher walks around the circle, initiating everyone in turn.

In the Great Pyramid people crawl through passageways. By having people walk upright with their feet touching the ground during the meditation, it helps keep people grounded. The understanding and wisdom that the YOD initiation brings comes with an effort. That is the reason why climbing the steps involves a bit of work.

EXPERIENCES OF MARY K HAYDEN OF IRELAND: The highlights of the meditation happened when we went down into the pyramid. With the priestess and priest, people came to us for healing, which we quietly did. The people simply appeared and disappeared. When we went to the King's Chamber, there was a golden glow around

Osiris — very powerful. When the power came through the crystal at the top of the pyramid it was like receiving an initiation down and through the body. I was very deep because I don't remember all of it right now. It was very sacred.

The YOD initiation was a lovely feeling of not just healing but beauty and power and holiness. There was a feeling of a great gift being bestowed upon me. It came with great comfort.

EXPERIENCE OF DORTHY OF NORTH CAROLINA, WHO DID NOT WISH TO HAVE HER REAL NAME USED: I was immediately dressed in Egyptian clothing. There were three priestesses; one's name was Jena and my name was Jeseriaha. The high priestess' name vacillated between Rata and Thoth. I asked how I knew Rata and I was told that I had been her son.

When we came to the sphinx, initially, I went to the right. Everything from there on in was a turn to the right. All of my questions were answered with, "You are here for healing.

In the Hall of the Animals I joined hands with everyone there and sent healing to the animals on Earth. The crystal bed in the Queen's Chamber felt like Larimar crystal. It was interesting that it was there. I kept soaking the energy up in all lifetimes - backwards and forwards and ongoing.

In the King's Chamber . . . I cannot remember it entirely. I do remember that all along the journey, I was dressed in Egyptian clothing and everyone else was as well. Climbing up the flights of stairs in the Great Pyramid was like climbing up the

Great Wall of China — doing so flexes all muscles in the body.

The YOD initiation came with no thunder - just gratitude.

EXPERIENCE OF DENISE OF THE NETHERLANDS: The priestess and priest were Maria and Jesus. The password was love. I felt like a little child. The initiation was lovely.

EXPERIENCE OF TRUDY VAN DER JAGT OF THE NETHERLANDS: The priestess was an old friend named Shiva. The priest, Pilot, was a big, powerful man. Both had straight black hair. They were wearing blue and gold. The first statue was a crocodile. I told the second statue, "I come to understand more about the YOD initiation. In Isis' chamber I felt warmth on the back of my body and a lot of power. During the initiation there was a lot of energy above my head.

EXPERIENCES OF PATRICIA ROSEBOOM OF THE NETHERLANDS: Anna and Pete were the priestess and priest. The password was dolphin. During the meditation I always turned left. During the initiation I was very deep and do not remember it.

EXPERIENCE OF JOAO RAMOS OF PORTUGAL: Everything in the meditation felt real and physical, as if I was really there. Sheban and Saba were the priestess and priest. During the initiation I saw yellow.

EXPEIENCES OF FRANK OF THE NETHERLANDS: Lilah was the priestess. I saw a lot of purple. The crystal bed was peaceful. In the King's Chamber I saw the image of Buddha. During the initiation, there was lots of white light.

EXPERIENCES OF VICKIE EBERLEIN OF GEORGIA: When I saw Isis, she was an off-colored, white horse with a very beautiful mane.

EXPERIENCES OF DONNIE HUNTER OF GEORGIA: When I met the priestess, she placed something on my head. When I met the priest, he and the priestess both drew something in my hands. I could feel it in my physical hands as they were drawing. In the crystal room I noticed that my feet were bound in chains. Isis broke it. For some reason I kept wanting to put them back on, but I kept reminding myself, *the chains are gone.* The stairs were tremendously high. I went up one step at a time — some steps were smaller; others were huge. My heart chakra is really open and moving now.

INSTRUCTOR: Change is difficult. What is familiar is comfortable, even if it harms us. In the Otherworlds it is possible to get to the root cause of repeated negative behaviors. The chains were a visual metaphor of what has been holding you back. As you relax into an easier way of walking or going forward, the old memories of the chain will disappear.

EXPERIENCES OF RYAN ALLEN NEAL OF FLORIDA: I felt like I was leaving old habits and feelings behind. When I went to the black statue, he told me that there was no password and sent me on. With the stairs, I felt like I was getting quite a workout. I reached Isis' room without a problem. The crystals were full of healing and happy energy. Osiris' room was warm. The power in the room had a comfortable feeling. During the initiation I felt a warm, pleasant feeling.

EXPERIENCES OF DOMINIKA KULIGOWSKA OF POLAND: The light changed all of the time from being more to less intense. I remember the password at the black figure; it was silence. In Isis' room I found a big, quartz crystal. I was told to embrace it and keep the energy inside. During the initiation, I felt a light around my head and a cool wind.

EXPERIENCES OF ANTHONY TORRES OF GEORGIA: The priestess stated that her name was Isis; the priest was Babaji. I took the passageway to the right. When I got to the black statue, he asked me what the password was. I answered, "It is my will!'

When the pink statue asked me a question, automatically the words came out of my mouth, "Light equals 93 equals will equals destiny."

When we got to the big, huge stairs, Isis and Babaji held my hands and levitated. As I climbed these huge, difficult steps, they pulled me along. When I got into the chambers of Isis, I laid down upon the quartz crystal bed. Waves of light came out of the bed and into me. Then I rolled over on my stomach for a while. In the King's Chamber I sat down in the chair - the armrests came over my arms. Then the chair started spinning fast. I couldn't comprehend the speed of it. During the initiation I felt activity and motion in the upper regions of my body.

Upperworld – the Realm of Angels and Spirits of the Departed

The Upperworld also has beautiful places in nature. It's not that the angels and souls of the departed do not help out in the Underworld, they do! However, it is the Upperworld that is considered to be their realm.

There are several ways to get to the Upperworld. In many cultures the Shaman journeys into the Underworld first. After finding her/his power animal, he asks the power animal to take her/him to the Upperworld. When s/he reaches the veil that separates this world from the Upperworld, s/he looks for an opening in the veil. Upon finding it s/he asks her/his power animal to guard the opening. When s/he has finished exploring the Upperworld, the Shaman comes back to the opening and asks the power animal to bring her/him back to where s/he started.

The Celts had another way of traveling to the Upperworld. The Shaman went into the World Tree and climbed the branches into the Upperworld. In modern times, people have taken the rainbow or flown through a stargate. Whichever way presents itself to the Shaman, the best advise is to simply go with it and keep going up. Sometimes, an aspiring Shaman will start going up one way, but decides s/he wants to go up

another way. Usually, the angels will take
the opportunity to teach the Shaman a
lesson by departing, leaving the Shaman
stuck in a light meditation going nowhere
for the remainder of the drumming. The
angels are reminding the aspiring Shaman
that the intention is set before the
journey and the details are left to the
angels. As with the Underworld, the Shaman
may ask questions in the Upperworld.

On the way to the Upperworld it is
rare but it sometimes happens that the
Shaman passes through a parade of floating,
square platforms. Each platform appears to
have its own dress code, as well as its own
unique symbols, which are etched on the
floor and sometimes worn as jewelry by the
inhabitants of the platform. The platforms
have neither walls nor ceilings; they are
open-air facilities. They all have pillars
at each of the corners; some have pillars
along the boarders of the platform. The
first time a Shaman sees such structures,
s/he may consider it to be a hallucination
because nobody will acknowledge or speak to
the Shaman. Absolutely nobody! However, it
is not that the platform inhabitants are
rude; they simply don't see the Shaman.
These souls are neither sad nor happy.
They could step off the platform at
anytime. However, it is as if they do not
know that they have the ability to do so.
As the Shaman journeys upwards, s/he
is able to see the whole picture. There are
many platforms below traveling in
concentric circles. Only those souls on the
innermost platforms show any signs of
concern, as the circle they travel in
becomes smaller and tighter. An outsider,

such as the Shaman, may wonder if these souls see the other platforms.

Who are these souls? In life they believed that their religious viewpoint was the only one. In death they cling tenaciously to their earthly values, as a dog to a bone.

Is there a way out? Only when the soul comes to the point where s/he asks, "Is there something else?"

It is as Jesus spoke, "Ask and you shall find; knock and the door shall be opened."

INSTRUCTOR: This is like the last journey you went on. It will also last for twenty minutes. When I begin beating the drum you will see yourself clearly in your mind's eye standing in a beautiful place in nature. You will find a way to the Upperworld. Your objective is to explore the Upperworlds. When you reach the Upperworld you may ask an angel to guide you, or you may find a deceased relative or friend to assist you. Among the many places of interest are places of healing, the angelic choir and the Akashic Records, which is like a library. It contains the true history of all who have lived, and God's Plan for Mother Earth.

You get to ask questions! When I change the beat of the drum, it is time to come back. If you are in the middle of something please finish what you are doing and then come back. You will return the same way you went down."

EXPERIENCES OF MARY K HAYDEN OF IRELAND: I saw a golden pole. Then it changed into steps. I walked up the golden steps to a veil or a cloud. Archangel

Zadkiel greeted me and led me through the veil or cloud or curtain — stepping from one reality into the next. Immediately, there was beautiful angelic music. My parents were the first to welcome me. Then lots of deceased family and friends greeted me. They were really excited. They put their hands out — everyone wanted to touch me and tell me that they were glad to see me.

INSTRUCTOR: Could it be that these souls are taking the Shamanic class with you?

MARY K HAYDEN: I am getting chills up and down my spine. The souls told me that I was helping them with their healing and that healing is the right path. So, that would really confirm that they are taking this class.

Archangel Michael was to the right-hand side of me with his blue sword giving me his blessing. Sometimes, I see it as red, but today it was blue. All of the edges around him were a luminescent blue. He pointed to literally a choir of thousands and thousands of angels. The music was amazing.

Then a young woman, who I never met, came to me. She was the niece of a friend, and she had been brutally murdered. She asked me to believe and let people know that the way she was portrayed in the media was not the way she was. She had rejected the man who murdered her because she realized he had been nothing but lies.

Then I found golden forms like golden eggs. I was told that they were miscarried and aborted babies. Their souls want to shine through. What do you think?

110

INSTRUCTOR: Did you tell them that they can be reborn?

MARY K HAYDEN: No I didn't.

INSTRUCTOR: If you wish, you may do that when we do a healing for the middle world.

MARY K HAYDEN: I think that they are teaching me about motherhood. I married a widower who already had children and I have not had any of my own.
After the small, golden souls, Archangel Michael brought me back to Zadkiel. Zadkiel handed me a note that said "Nice!"

INSTRUCTOR: When words are spoken and the listener or even the speaker gets the chills, it is a confirmation that the truth has been spoken. This type of psychic perception is called clairsentience. It is possible because the truth is always clear and uncomplicated. While you are in the class, your spirit guides and those you knew who have passed on have the opportunity to take the class as well. As you receive initiations, the angels initiate the spirits in the room.

EXPERIENCE OF DOROTHY OF NORTH CAROLINA, WHO DID NOT WISH TO HAVE HER REAL NAME USED: I like to go down to the Underground, so I went onto a slide and then upward and out to the Upperworld. I came to a mountainous region. Waited to see angels, but they did not appear. I felt that I was with the ascended masters and decided to just enjoy it. First the Star of David appeared; it was very pronounced.

111

Then the symbol, Merkaba, came and spun before my eyes. I then held hands with the Ascended Masters and asked for forgiveness. I forgave myself.

I wasn't feeling comfortable because I wasn't feeling anything. Then I was on the back of white buffalo, but then he was bucking, so, I decided to get off.

INSTRUCTOR: Next time, rather than you deciding how to get to the Upperworld, watch yourself and see what happens. Likewise, rather than you deciding what to do when something uncomfortable happens ask why it is happening. If you are still uneasy with the answer, you have the choice to leave. However, even though White Buffalo was bucking, you were safe. Maybe he was trying to release dark energy? You won't know unless you ask in the moment.

DOROTHY: Do spirits have as easy a time as healing as we do?

INSTRUCTOR: No, it is harder to resolve issues or heal in the spiritual world. It is one reason why suicide for the purpose of escaping issues in this world is counterproductive. Souls on the Otherside of the Veil are certainly helped by prayers from the living. It is also possible for someone with healing energy to send them healing. This is doable because the boundaries between this world and the next are an illusion, and also because God's Spirit permeates everything.

EXPERIENCE OF DENISE OF THE NETHERLANDS: I was guided to a beautiful park. I didn't want the drumming to stop.

EXPERIENCE OF TRUDY VAN DER JAGT OF THE NETHERLANDS: I went up Jacob's ladder. I was laughing with Saint Peter, who gave me a tour. I saw the souls of those waiting to be reborn; they were talking with angels and planning their next life. There were lots of angels singing. I met my grandmother and spent some time with her. When I asked to see the Akashic Records, I was shown a huge field.

EXPERIENCES OF PATRICIA ROSEBOOM OF THE NETHERLANDS: I stood by myself. Nobody came!

INSTRUCTOR: It could be that you needed to rest or that you were not ready to go to the Upperworlds yet. You may always try again.

EXPERIENCE OF JOAO RAMOS OF PORTUGAL: I tried to go but couldn't. Instead, I found my father, who had not gone to the Light. With the angels we opened the vortex and sent him up. I stayed with the drumming. The colors were amazing. There is quiet in my head.

EXPEIENCES OF FRANK OF THE NETHERLANDS: I fell asleep. The drumming at the end woke me up.

EXPERIENCES OF VICKIE EBERLEIN OF GEORGIA: To get to the Upperworld I went down the shaft to the bottom. I asked an animal to help me to get up to the Upperworld, but I got lost and asked for a spirit guide to help me. He came and yanked me into the Upperworld, just as someone might yank a child off the ground.

When I reached the Upperworld, a broom with a pentagram hanging on it was waiting for me. On one side of the broom it was night and on the other it was daylight. We were just flying around doing loops when we came to what looked like a very large stained-glass window with light shining through it. It was very beautiful. Then I realized that it was a very large crystal. As I stood watching it, the light through the crystal came together to form a pink ball. I was told that I needed to get a pink crystal. I asked if there was healing for me there.

Suddenly, everything changed colors and everything was shapes. I came to another crystal that was like liquid light. I asked if I could go inside. When I was inside the crystal I looked out at all of the beings that inhabited this world going about their business. The dragons were gentle, and there were angelfish flying through the air. Then I came back to the drum. Whenever it changed, it would swirl me into the sound.

INSTRUCTOR: Pentagrams are symbols of protection; that's why black magicians stand in the middle of them.

EXPERIENCES OF DONNIE HUNTER OF GEORGIA: The animal that took me to the Upperworld was an enormous, long-necked dragon. He had an amazing wingspan with fire-red on the edges of his wings. He picked me up with his claws, but then I was riding on its back. I wasn't afraid; I was very comfortable. He dropped me off on some rocks outside of a gorgeous city.

Then I found myself hovering above, looking at myself in the middle of a circle of healers. There was an old medicine woman; her age and wisdom went beyond records. She had beads and feathers in her hair, and a shawl wrapped around her back and under her arms. She was waving some kind of a fan over my head and torso. She chanted some words when she was on my right side. When she came around to my left side she blew in my ear. A muscle in my head became extremely hot.

Then I found myself on the beach. I heard a horse whiney. Then a cowboy on a horse approached me. He asked me to join him for a ride in the sky. I got on a horse, but I found myself riding backwards. To my left were hundreds of horses and riders. The sky was beautiful shades of grays and blues. Every now and then a tree or rock would go quickly by. The speed at which we were traveling was far beyond comprehension.

When other people are talking about their journeys, I can see what they are describing taking place. It's like a movie in my head. Why is that?

INSTRUCTOR: On your journey into the Otherworlds you work with spiritual beings who have spiritual gifts. If you want to have spiritual gifts, hang out with those who have them. Journeying into the Otherworlds is a way to build psychic abilities. Communicating psychically is the language of the spiritual world. When a Shaman returns from a journey into the Otherworlds, s/he recounts her/his journey using her/his psychic impressions. This imagery carries an energy, which creates vibrant movies in the third eye of the listener. It is the stuff of folktales!

To go one step further, the afterlife is the real reality; an earthwalk is an illusion. However, each incarnation has the potential to be a powerful dream, during which we are given opportunities to learn, work through lessons, grow, enjoy and love. Spiritual gifts are not the end of the journey; rather, they are a means to an end if used correctly.

EXPERIENCES OF RYAN ALLEN NEAL OF FLORIDA: I was standing there waiting for whatever it was that was going to pick me up. A light came down. There was a being in the light. He grabbed my hand and up we went. We arrived at what looked like a busy place. We wandered around until we came to Earth. Half of the Earth was scorched, and the other half was a beautiful light. I was told that it was OK. Then these corks went into the scorched side. As the corks went into the Earth they spun faster and faster and faster until the scorched side was gone — completely gone. Then this great being put his hand around the world, and the Earth became whole and beautiful. I asked, "What does this mean?"

I heard, "There has to be cleansing of the world. It is inevitable that we are going to experience half of the world gone!"

After that I just went through space, visited some planets and then came back here.

INSTRUCTOR: In the original writings of the Disciples, which have been turned into the New Testament, Jesus did not predict the end of the world at this time. Jesus stated that there would be a time of disruption and earth changes before the

116

Golden Age is established on Earth. Nostradamas predicted the same thing, as did the Mayan, Egyptian, Aztec and Egyptian prophets. Noah's Ark is the story of another time when Earth went through a cleansing. At the end of the story God promises that the whole world will never be destroyed again. Nostradamas predicted the deaths of Jack and Robert Kennedy and said that these events were inevitable. Both Nostradamas and Jesus stated that the time of chaos before the Golden Age could be made as dramatic or as easy as humanity wished. So, when we campaign for environmental or human rights causes, and against war, or go into the Otherworlds to do healings for Mother Earth, we are lending a hand in easing the destructive natural forces of Earth.

EXPERIENCES OF DOMINIKA KULIGOWSKA OF POLAND: I went back to the liquid light in the forest. I asked, "How do I get to the Upperworld?" My angel came and we flew very fast. When I got to the Upperworld I could not see any objects, just glowing haze everywhere. Then I saw many angels; they had a lot of light inside. They were different colors, and they had different responsibilities. I was only observing them. Then I saw a master and he just nodded. What I understood was that this was a place I could go to when I meditated. In the background I saw some big letters, which said "HOME".

EXPERIENCES OF ANTHONY TORRES OF GEORGIA: It started with a bird, who was a combination of a hummingbird and bluebird. It looked down at me with a commanding look. Then the little, baby bluebird morphed into

117

a huge, powerful, intense dragon. He gave me a smile and I got on him. We rode around for quite a while. We left a wooded area and into a blank space. I asked him what this was. He answered, "This is the part of the holographic universe that has not been filled in yet — it would be called the future."

The vast white went on until we came to spiraling vortexes that lined up. I started flying! The dragon looked at me and asked, "What are you doing?" I realized that I did not have any intention.

He took me to an orange, castle-like house. Cobalt blue emanated from it. It was just there, not on the ground. I walked into the house to find only one room with one long, wooden table and three Merlin-type wizards sitting around it. They were talking about things that needed to take place. I asked, "Why am I here?"

One wizard answered sternly, "For you to take the next step in your initiation and experience you must have a total shift in perception. For the next consecutive 30 days you must recognize the absolute light within 33 people and not see them from the perception of their body and personality." I left the house and rode the dragon. I felt the changes in atmosphere as I was coming back.

SHAMANIC II: In the Shamanic II class the students are asked to go into the Upperworld as the Celts journeyed. The Celts envisioned themselves in a beautiful place in nature and found the World Tree. Then s/he would find an opening in the Tree and travel through the branches to the Upperworld.

INSTRUCTOR: When I begin beating the drum you will see yourself clearly in your mind's eye standing in a beautiful place in nature. Look for the World Tree and find an opening. Go into an aperture and travel up the branches of the Tree. You will come out in the Upperworld. You may find yourself in a beautiful place in nature, or surrounded by a beautiful white light, which emanates a loving presence.

EXPERIENCE OF LENA LIDMALM OF SWEDEN: I saw the right eye and nose of an old man. It disappeared and I went into the Tree and up the branches. I asked, "How do I use my wings?"

I was told, "Nobody wants to tell you. You have to find out for yourself."

I let go and leaped off of the Tree. After I flew around for a while, I landed and lay on the ground. I looked up and saw buildings in the sky. Then the buildings went poof and disappeared.

EXPERIENCE OF ANGELA JOHANSSON OF SWEDEN: I ended up on a big mountain. I was told that if I wanted to, that I could fly. So, I flew like a small pink butterfly. Within myself it was like I could feel soft rain.

EXPERIENCE OF ANDREAS BLOMBERG OF SWEDEN: Transformation from Formula 1 to the top of the Tree! I saw myself with wings and I could fly. It wasn't easy. There were clouds and I saw some people. I asked who they were but did not receive a clear answer.

EXPERIENCE OF HANNI BLOMBERG OF SWEDEN: I came up to a big tree with fruit on it. I went up so fast; the power of the tree took me up. I used my wings and flew. I played with a bird. Angels above me were laughing, "There's a beginner!" I flew up to them. They said, "You must be graceful, like a dancer." They taught me how to come down. Swish, straight down!

FIRST ENOCHIAN MAGIC INITIATION GIVEN IN THE FIRST SHAMANIC CLASS: The initiation symbol is given at the third eye, into the etheric solar plexus and on the soles of the feet. It is a magical initiation in that the initiator figuratively opens the etheric channels of the initiate and balances the energy. The result being that whatever energy the initiate is channeling becomes much more. If the initiate is not channeling any healing energy then there is no difference.

The initiation described above is literally older than the hills. It has NOTHING whatsoever to do with the black magic system, which the black magicians named Enochian Magic. If the black magicians gave a true name of what their magical system does, people would surely think twice before becoming involved. The following is an excerpt from Tera, My Journey Home:

John Dee was an astrologer. He picked the day for Queen Elizabeth I's coronation and instructed her in arcane matters. He was also suspected of being an espionage agent for the Queen and signed his correspondence to her "007", just like Ian Fleming's character, James Bond. John Dee was not psychic; he took notes! It was

Edward Kelley who perceived information from the Otherworlds during their scrying sessions. The 'angels' they were involved with, however, are highly suspect. The 'angels' gave the men both white and black magic - although the 'angels' did tell the men never to use the system of black magic. (What was the point of giving Dee and Kelley the black magic system?) Both Dee and Kelley had warnings that the whole system was corrupt when the 'angels' threatened to put a curse on John Dee and his progeny for five generations because he was not doing their bidding fast enough. The 'angels' also told Kelley that he had to get married even though Kelley didn't want to get married. Then the 'angels' told Dee and Kelley to swap wives. Interestingly, while Dee thought the 'angels' were genuine, Kelley, the psychic, felt that the 'angels' were deceiving them. Dee and Kelley worked together for five years and the Otherworld communication stopped when the two men parted. What was their part in the cult of the Queen and what part did magic play? Later, Aleister Crowley used Dee and Kelley's Enochian Magic for black magic.

EXAMPLE OF SOMEONE WHO USED KELLEY AND DEE'S SYSTEM: Ten years ago, Claire Campbell met a man who was practicing a black magic system called Enochian Magic. He told her that it worked. A few years ago, Claire met the same man. In those seven years she had not seen him, he had aged more than twenty years. His skin had a gray pallor; he was melancholy, bent and generally in ill health. While black magic may initially appear to be a shortcut; at the end of the day, we all receive by the power of ten whatever we do to others. This is one reason why Christ said, "Do unto others as you would have others do unto you!"

INSTRUCTOR: You will be initiated into the Enochian Magic initiation, which dates back to the Old Testament. I will call upon the priests and priestesses of the Order of Melchizedek, the Priest Melchizedek and the Fathers of Abraham to assist with the initiation. Some psychics feel that the Priest Melchizedek was one of Jesus' reincarnations. I will leave that question with you to figure out in the Otherworlds.

EXPERIENCES OF MARY K HAYDEN OF IRELAND: As soon as you stood in front of me, I could see a swirling rainbow. The center was like the eye of a storm. The energy was really powerful with all of the colors of the rainbow swirling around it. When you touched my feet, it felt like hot coals, almost like a branded steer might feel. It wasn't unpleasant, but very hot and very beautiful. Does that make sense?

INSTRUCTOR: Part of the lesson you learn in this class is to put your analytical mind aside so that the creative mind has an opportunity to express itself. Sensations experienced in initiations that come from another dimension may be illogical. However, when initiations produce desirable results then the left brain has to accept the conclusion that there is something else out there beside what can be seen, heard or felt in the physical world.

Once I did a healing on a man with kidney problems at a public healing demonstration in Ireland. He got so hot that he was sweating through his jacket. He told me that if he was running a temperature this hot that he'd be in the hospital. As the angels were in charge, the man was healed.

EXPERIENCE OF DOROTHY OF NORTH CAROLINA: The first thing that happened to me was that I became nauseous. Then peace came over me. It was just like the healing you did on me. Why is that?

INSTRUCTOR: Initiations can bring on a healing, or release of undesirable energies so that the energy of the initiation will take. You are still going through a healing process. That is, there was too much 'stuff' for you to let go of in the one private healing session you had with me. That is not uncommon. The next time you have an initiation or healing it may or may not be the same experience. While it is uncomfortable in the moment, 'stuff' is leaving.

DOROTHY: I had that same nauseous feeling in the barn today with your horses. I was being healed of negative thoughts that have been with me all of my life.

INSTRUCTOR: Negative thoughts are toxic and will make the physical body sick. As you release negative thoughts, your conscious mind and physical body become aware of how noxious they really are. It is also possible that your guides and angels want to make this clear to you.

DOROTHY: I know that I have been trying to release these thoughts for many, many lifetimes. It's interesting to see how these thoughts permeate every cell of my body. My mother died from them. Of course, I have my mother's thoughts.

INSTRUCTOR: Your mother has passed, is that correct?

DOROTHY: Yes!

INSTRUCTOR: I bet that your mother is here going through the healing process with you!

DOROTHY (smiling): As you said the words, I just got that very strongly. I guess I am doing this class for myself, my daughter and my mother.

EXPERIENCE OF DENISE OF THE NETHERLANDS: I felt more energy, especially after you initiated my feet.

EXPERIENCES OF PATRICIA ROSEBOOM OF THE NETHERLANDS: When you were at my solar plexus, I could feel the angels working on me.

EXPERIENCE OF JOAO RAMOS OF PORTUGAL: I still feel the initiation.

EXPERIENCES OF VICKIE EBERLEIN OF GEORGIA: I was surprised by how strong the energy felt coming out of the bottom of my feet. Watching the energy coming out of my fingertips was fascinating.

INSTRUCTOR: Now that your feet are open, you will be able to release toxicity out through them more easily, and pull up more healing energy from the Earth.

EXPERIENCES OF DONNIE HUNTER OF GEORGIA: I could feel the energy as you approached me. I have felt energy before but this is hard to describe. I could feel you pulling the energy in everyone you initiated. I feel as though I won the lottery.

EXPERIENCES OF ANTHONY TORRES OF GEORGIA: The experience was indescribable.

SECOND ENOCHIAN MAGIC INITIATION GIVEN IN THE SECOND SHAMANIC CLASS: This initiation is given in the aura over the shoulder blades, on the third eye and in the palms of the hands. In addition, the initiator works through the aura to open the etheric channels. At the shoulder blades, many initiates feel as if they have wings of light after the attunement.

EXPERIENCE OF LENA LIDMALM OF SWEDEN: There was a strong pressure across my forehead. Then I saw a big, bright light and a flying heart. I feel calm.

EXPERIENCE OF ANGELA JOHANSSON OF SWEDEN: My experiences were exactly the same as Lena, but I saw drops of water.

EXPERIENCE OF ANDREAS BLOMBERG OF SWEDEN: Sometimes, I felt heat. Most of the time, I felt nothing. Hanni tells me that my hands are very hot and powerful when I am healing her, but I feel nothing.

125

INSTRUCTOR: Sometimes, healers do not feel anything during the laying on of hands. I believe that God does this intentionally so as to keep us humble. Also, healings may occur on many dimensions, and the complexity of how angels and other holy spirits go about healing is beyond human comprehension. The most important thing is not that healers feel the energy or even that the client feels the energy. The most important thing is that healings occur.

EXPERIENCE OF HANNI BLOMBERG OF SWEDEN: My experience was similar to Lena's and Angela's. However, instead of pressure, I felt heat at my third eye, electricity around me, and pressure in my heart was released. I don't know if I saw drops of water, or if they were stars. My hands were very warm during the initiation. I knew that the initiation was special. My hands are still warm.

EXPERIENCE OF WILLEM BOEREN OF THE NETHERLANDS: My back felt very warm and there is tingling and energy in my hands. I feel that the energy is grounded in me.

EXPERIENCE OF MARIAN VALKENBURGH OF THE NETHERLANDS: At my head I saw circles. Then my head expanded. My back is loose, my hands are tingling and I feel more grounded.

EXPERIENCE OF JOAO RAMOS OF PORTUGAL: At first, it was cold and then I became warm. A pressure at my 3rd eye was released. My hands have lots of energy in them.

Shaman's Death – Dying to Old Fears

When humans first appeared on Earth, cavemen were primarily concerned with survival — issues regarding sustenance and continuance of the group. In living close to and dependant upon nature, they learned to listen to the consciousness of the world around them. Thus, they learned to work with nature so as to insure their survival. Before a hunt, they found that if they appealed to the consciousness of the animal they hunted, hunting was more successful. They discovered that when they thanked the animals afterwards, more bounty came to them. Groups of humans who did not learn to do this did not survive.

At some point, a few people were born with more psychic abilities. They were able to see and speak to spirits and to the departed. When these spirits told a psychic that a herd would be in a specific place at a certain time of day, and the hunters followed the message, the hunters discovered the animals exactly as they had been predicted. Because of the psychics' accuracy, they became respected. With respect, a psychic's status in the community evolved. A Shaman's or psychic's ability to communicate with the departed gave reassurance to the members of the tribe that personality survived death, just as it does today.

To help the dying go through the death process and help the spirit of the departed navigate through the Middleworld, the Shaman gave the dying individual imagery to look for that would help her/him make a successful transition. Eventually, these visual metaphors became a roadmap to whatever the tribe called the afterlife or heaven. As was mentioned earlier, an Egyptian expected that after death, her/his soul would travel safely with Anubis. While the imagery in cultures throughout the world differs, the message is the same — personality survives death and moves on to another world.

Death of a Shaman does not involve a physical death of any kind. Early on, the Shaman discovered that when s/he cleared her/himself of old fears, her/his psychic and healing abilities increased. To achieve this cleansing, the Shaman would journey into the Underworld and look for something to eat her/him. The image of her/himself did not represent the Shaman's physical body or soul. Instead, the representation of self embodied the Shaman's deepest fears. In many cultures, during the journey of the Death of a Shaman, the Shaman was eaten feet first. There is no pain other than completely surrendering to that which is feared the most. After the Shaman was completely consumed and released from that which ate her/him, the Shaman would search for a new body. Traditionally, this body was built from the bones outwards. When their new body was constructed, the Shaman returned to consciousness.

The following experience will give you some idea that what to expect is the unexpected. Gisela took the Shamanic I class many years ago. Shamanic journeys, especially those that impact lives profoundly, may be recalled much later with vivid remembrance.

EXPERIENCE OF GISELA HAMMERSTEIN OF AGRENTINA: Dear Kathleen, As I am translating your book (Tera, My Journey Home: Alternative Healing) into Spanish I became absolutely attached to your horse, Bucky. I remembered the experience I had during Death of a Shaman. When I went to the Underworld I found my biggest fear in a cave and went through it. When I started to come back I found Bucky in the entrance of the cave. I got on his back and he galloped away. I held onto his neck with both of my arms. In his neck he had an amazing amount of fear (from horrendous abuse and neglect). Then there appeared a big crocodile in front of us. He was so vivid then that I can still see the crocodile now. My sense then and now is that the crocodile was very old. Bucky wanted to stop and return to the back of the cave, but I encouraged him to go on. I told Bucky that I would be going through the crocodile with him and would stay with him through the entire process. As we progressed forwards and into the jaws of the beast, I constantly whispered into Bucky's ears, "Everything will be fine!"

Bucky struggled with his fear. I could feel it in his body under my legs and arms. When the crocodile had finished eating us, Bucky received his new body and happily cantered to the cave entrance and into the Underworld. When we came back to where I started the journey, the Earth was shining in her marvelous splendor. I got off Bucky and he joined the other horses, who were

129

waiting for him. We had both received a profound healing.

Your newsletter is always like a song from the heart. Love, Giesela

KATHLEEN: If fears are deep-seated issues from another lifetime, then the animal or thing that eats the Shaman may appear old or worn.

As a follow up to Bucky: Bucky is a Saddlebred who was abused, rehabilitated, stolen, re-abused, neglected and returned to me through the judicial system. Many horses, who go through severe trauma, are never able to be fully rehabilitated; most remain unridable. When Bucky was returned to me, his body was vacant; his personality was gone. It took Bucky many years to release his fears. The Death of a Shaman journey and the subsequent feeling of peace and joy that Gisela and Bucky experienced has taken years to manifest.

Early in 2005, I realized that my wellspring of inspiration had dried up, and that in order to rediscover and motivate my creative brain, I had to move. In May of 2005, my horses, cats and myself moved to the lush, green countryside of North Carolina from the deserts of Arizona. Of my four horses, Bucky had never been turned out in a large pasture before. When he was turned out for the first time in North Carolina, it was as if he was thinking *I never imagined anything like this existed.* While the pasture and grazing was extremely healing for him, the surroundings were completely foreign. This in itself brought up more fears to be released and healed.

Once in New York I did a Shamanic journey for Danuska's thoroughbred mare, who was pregnant with twins. For those of you who are not familiar with horses, a horse fetus must be carried to full term by the mare. The likelihood of twins being carried the entire eleven months of a horse's pregnancy is doubtful. Aborting a pregnancy in a mare is dangerous. During this particular healing journey, I simply watched the angels as they worked. Up until the colt was born in January, the veterinarian heard three heartbeats — the mother and the two fetuses. However, when the foal was born, there was only one. A very sudden and dramatic healing occurred at the time of birth! So, whether it is Death of a Shaman or another type of journey, sometimes, changes occur immediately. Other times, such as in Bucky's case, a lengthy process is involved.

To give you further examples of Death of a Shaman, here is an excerpt from Tera, My Journey Home: Alternative Healing:

I have been studying Shamanism longer than I have studied Reiki. I went through this ceremony years ago and was surprised when darkness ate me. Since then, I have been releasing my fear of small, enclosed, dark places as well as my fear of working with the Great Void that is found within. From my Shamanic Workshop students, I have discovered that this fear often comes from past lives where we were burned alive or otherwise tortured for being a witch. In my classes I explain Death of a Shaman and then give them a break, allowing them the freedom of choice as to whether or not they are ready to journey Death of a Shaman. I typically hear my students telling other people, whom they find in the hallway, "We are going to be eaten!" I could write a whole chapter or perhaps even a book on my students' experiences, but I will give a few examples.

A clergyman in New York returned from Death of a Shaman with this tale. He had gone into the Underworld searching for something to eat him. He ran into a handsome young man, who asked him what he was doing. The clergyman responded, "I am looking for something to eat me."
With that, the handsome young man turned into the devil, frightened the clergyman, and then proceeded to eat him. When the devil was through, he turned back into a handsome young man again and the clergyman got a new body.

Edde Sailer went into the Underworld to find something to eat her and found a snake, who ate her whole. As she was passing through the body of the snake, she became frightened, but she remembered that I had instructed them that they could call upon their power animals, angels or other Holy Spirits to help them or to answer questions. In the belly of the snake, Edde called out to her guide to ask why it was taking so long. Her guide responded, "It's all right! Relax! I am right here!"

Edde did as her guide instructed, came out, got a new body and came back to consciousness.

Ian went into the Underworld, but rather than looking for something to eat him, he decided that he would take on anything that tried to eat him. Ian was successful because nothing in the Underworld can make the Shaman do anything that he does not want to do. The only exception is for those individuals who work with demons in black magic rituals - in the Underworld, these entities control the Shaman. I have had one such student who came to the conscious realization after journeying that these demons also controlled him in his consciousness. Getting back to Ian! After a while, Ian got tired of chasing off his fears, and he asked his guide, "What is it that I am learning from this?"

He was told, "Nothing!" So, Ian consented to be eaten. With that a large bird snatched him up, flew very high in the sky and then dropped him. Ian landed on his head, which split open. All kinds of ugly, rotten things came out. Then an array of insects and reptiles consumed him. He got a new body and returned to consciousness visibly shaken, but with conscious clarity of mind.

Evelyn Kerns' journeys belong in a class all by themselves. Evelyn went into the Underworld, but no one or nothing would eat her. She was about to give up hope when she ran into a cartoon-type, Puff the Magic Dragon creature, but he told her he was afraid she wouldn't taste very good. Evelyn offered to pour honey over herself, but he still didn't think he would eat her. When she asked him what would make her palatable, the dragon pondered and said that maybe if she doused herself in mustard, he could swallow her whole. Evelyn obliged, she was eaten and then she proceeded to poke him from inside. He jumped up and down. Then he expelled her and she floated out whole inside of an iridescent bubble.

INSTRUCTOR: When I begin beating the drum you will see yourself clearly in your mind's eye standing in a beautiful place in nature. You will find an opening into the Underworld. When you reach the Underworld you will look for something to eat you. It is NOT painful. You are NOT killing your body or your spirit. Your intention in Death of a Shaman is to die to that which you fear. Do NOT decide on your own what it is you fear. Focus on yourself and see what happens. Typically, you are eaten from the feet to the head. Remember, you get to ask questions! Ask them! After you have been eaten you will come out. At this point, you will find your body or it will be re-created from the bones out. Some people find this so liberating that they look around for something else to eat them.

EXPERIENCES OF MARY K HAYDEN OF IRELAND: My very friendly big brown bear ate me. That in itself was quite a shock because he is my power animal. The good thing was that I was very familiar with him. When I initially went into the Underworld we talked, and I said, "I didn't expect to see you here!"

He said, "Well, you have lessons to learn."

I had contradictory feelings. For in some way it was comforting being in his hands. He started with my head and then tore my limbs. It all seemed to be in slow motion. I looked down and saw bits of myself being digested. I did not know that I had any deep-seated fear. He told me, "Everyone who looks cuddly is not friendly."

My body was just lying asleep waiting for me and I slipped back into it. I felt that he showed me his two sides. Mother nature is Mother Nature, and we all have our instincts. Enlightening and a serious reminder!

EXPERIENCE OF DOROTHY OF NORTH CAROLINA, WHO DID NOT WANT TO HAVE HER REAL NAME USED: An alligator ate me. Of course I asked why and he said, "Because I am suppose to eat you."

He started to eat me rapidly head first, but I told him that he had to eat me feet first. So, I came out and he proceeded again. He took his time; I had prolonged the feast. Then it went quickly. I came out and was thrown out into another world. I was looking for my body. I saw a butterfly and then hawks and eagles and little birds that I did not recognize. An owl came and I became the owl.

INSTRUCTOR: You figured out for yourself that sometimes things do not go exactly as planned, and by taking control of the situation rather than asking "why?" additional difficulties are created. Your lesson is applicable to all journeys in the Otherworlds. When in doubt ask questions.

EXPERIENCE OF TRUDY VAN DER JAGT OF THE NETHERLANDS: A horse ate me. It was quickly done! I asked, "What is my fear?"
"Fear of being assertive!"

EXPERIENCE OF DENISE OF THE NETHERLANDS: Yesterday, I felt nothing in Death of a Shaman and could not find anyone to eat me.
I must tell you that I am always afraid of riding in a car on the highway. Fast speeds bother me, and I sit very tense in the car. This morning on the way to class, I was surprised that I was relaxed. My husband turned to me and wanted to know what had happened to me.

EXPERIENCES OF PATRICIA ROSEBOOM OF THE NETHERLANDS: Also, I was eaten by a horse and my own dog. I have been a little afraid of horses. As for my dog, I am afraid that he's going to die.

EXPERIENCE OF JOAO RAMOS OF PORTUGAL: I started to go down. This time, it was slippery. When I reached the bottom, a dinosaur waited for me. I slid right into his mouth.

EXPEIENCES OF FRANK OF THE NETHERLANDS: It started with termites eating my legs. A spider ate my heart. Other insects came to eat me and then I went into a snake. I had to laugh!

EXPERIENCES OF VICKIE EBERLEIN OF GEORGIA: Lots of things wanted to eat me; they were all volunteering. I went into an alien. I ended up in a birthing canal and came out on top of a mountain. A turtle met me and he wanted to become my new body but he was too small. The turtle asked me to throw him into the air so that he might become larger. I was looking around and a demon appeared. He ate me in one gulp. I came out the end of his tail. I have always been uncomfortable in small, dimly lit places. So, the next thing to eat me was darkness.

EXPERIENCES OF DONNIE HUNTER OF GEORGIA: When I started out I had a hard time finding an animal to eat me. A bear came and took a huge bit out of my side. I told him that he was doing it the wrong way; he was supposed to start with my feet and work up. He kept chewing and chewing on my ribs and liver. Finally, I said, "I'm sorry but this isn't going to work."

I patted bear on the head and said, "Would you mind leaving?"

So, I went on my merry way and found an industrial tree shredder — the machines they feed large branches into, and spits out millions of pieces of wood. I jumped in feet first. All of the way down I thought, "Yes, this is it!" I remember holding my hands up as I went through, just like the people on the waterslide who are rushing down a steep incline. I could see the two big rollers come right up over my head. Somewhere, while going through the machine, I turned around and I came out headfirst. I felt the air, landed on the ground, got up and walked off with a beautiful, white body.

I listened to the drum for a few minutes, and then I was told, "You have one more! You have to be run over by a truck. It has to be in California on the 405!"

So, I found myself riding with my best friend in the cab of a large truck. I asked him, "Would you do me a favor? If I get out and stand on the highway, would you just run me over?"

He said, "Are you serious?"

I said, "Yes! Just don't worry about it?"

"You won't be mad?"

"No, I'm not going to be mad."

So, I stand in the middle of the interstate and here he comes — going a hundred miles an hour. He hit me and I just exploded. Then I got another body.

INSTRUCTOR: The next time something happens that isn't what you expect, or different from the directions that were given before the journey, rather than you changing the situation, you might try asking, "Why is this happening in this way?" Or, "Why are you here?" Maybe the brown bear was to eat you as well? Maybe not? You will find the answers when you ask the question in the moment. However, sometimes the answers may not come immediately.

EXPERIENCES OF RYAN ALLEN NEAL OF FLORIDA: I waited a while for anything at all to come by. All of a sudden a spaceship appeared and took me up. The gray aliens didn't say anything. It felt as though I was riding with them for about ten minutes. Then they pushed a button and just dropped me into a huge pit. Then this huge praying mantis took its sweet time in taking me down. It spit me back out and I was pink. I floated to a rock and a bird picked me up and carried me across an ocean. We landed and he shredded me. I came together whole and as myself.

INSTRUCTOR: I used to have clients who came to me with abduction experiences by aliens in gray spacesuits. When I asked the angels how these people might be helped, the angels said, "If people will ask for or visualize cobalt blue before going to sleep at night, the nightmares and abductions will stop." I put this information into my first book, <u>Reiki & Other Rays of Touch Healing</u>, in a chapter entitled *Who are the Grays and Other Things that Go Bump in the Night.*

One day, a woman, who said that she had been the highest-ranking woman officer when she was in service, called. She told me that her son had had terrifying abduction experiences, even during the day. She told him about what I had written in the chapter. She also told him about one of the Universal Laws concerning honoring another's wishes, which is also mentioned in the book. One way to invoke this law is to state clearly when seeing spirit (any spirits), "If you have come in the name of Jesus, please stay, otherwise go away!"

When the Grays approached the woman's son, he shortened the statement to, "In the name of Jesus, go now!" It worked!

The only time this will not work is when an individual makes deep connections to evil forces through black magic or ignorance. The story of <u>The Exorcist</u> is a true story of a little boy in Chicago. It is not that the Ouija board was bad; it's that when the children made contact with a

139

spirit they did not know to use the above statement in order to check out who they were dealing with. Nor did they know how to clear the board if the spirit was negative.

Do I believe that people have been abducted? Some people are attention seekers; others are legitimate. Either way, the individual needs healing.

EXPERIENCES OF DOMINIKA KULIGOWSKA OF POLAND: I was eaten twice, first by a dragon. It was a very strange dragon; he was tall and had the mannerisms of an Englishman. We had a polite conversation and then he suggested, "You know I can help you with that if you want."

I said, "OK, Thank you very much for that!"

So, he started chewing me. It took a while. It was not painful at all. When he was through, I found myself lying on the ground. It took me a while to figure out that I was the grass. I could see parts of me and that I was green. Then I heard someone approaching. I saw that it was a goat, who looked very bored. He started eating me, and again it took a while.

EXPERIENCES OF ANTHONY TORRES OF GEORGIA: There were some sharks swimming by. They were aware that I was there. One came up and simply swallowed me whole. I came out and was swimming around again. Another shark got me in an extremely violent manner. He ripped me to shreds, and then he started eating the shreds. I came out of the shark and ended up on the ocean floor. I turned into a dolphin and started swimming with the sharks. I was not afraid of them; as a matter of fact, they were afraid of me. I was swimming very happily and decided to do a flip out of the water. At the top of my jump I dissipated into the stars. I stayed that way for a while. When I came back, all of the stars that I had created formulated into one force and came through. As it came down through the sky, I flashed into a bluebird, then into the dolphin at the peak of its jump, and then landed deftly on the ground as a human. I was proud of the way I landed and showing off. I felt strange and uneasy. Then three big, yellow birds with fangs appeared. They picked my body up. One grabbed half my body and the other two took a hold of each side. They all ate me, and then merged into one bird. I came out of the bird and landed on the ground as myself.

SHAMANIC II: In the Shamanic II class the students are asked to go to the World Tree and sit under it. Waiting in the branches of the World Tree is the Mother Bird. The following is an excerpt from Between Two Worlds: The Story of Henry VIII and Anne Boleyn — and Her Celtic Heritage:

Before her death, Lady Margaret shared secret arcane knowledge of the story of Ella of the Cinders; however, Anne had not done the journey. Anne now lay on her bed trembling with fear, recalling her grandmother's words. "In the top branches of the World Tree lives a great bird of prey that sometimes takes on female form. When she does, she is called the Old Bone Goddess. When a wisewoman is ready to surrender entirely to God and Goddess and die to everything that she holds onto, she goes into a trance state. Seeing herself, she journeys down the roots of the World Tree. Once in the Underworld, she calls for the large Mother Bird, who has great, sharp talons and a razor-like beak. The Mother Bird obliges by swooping down, tearing the flesh from her bones and distributing the pieces to creatures that the wisewoman fears the most. These creatures eat her body until only bones are left; the Bone Goddess gathers them up and places them in a caldron. Within a short time, the wisewoman rises from the caldron re-assembled. When the wisewoman is ready, the Old Bone Goddess returns to help her reincarnate. Ella of the Cinders is the Bone Goddess, as is the White Lady who comes for the dying. When the tiny will of man is surrendered to the Greater Will of God, then and only then will life be supportive, joyful and fulfilled."

Anne felt that everything she had done had gone amiss, everything with the exception of Princess Elizabeth. Her way had not worked; she was at last ready to surrender her will to the Greater Will. Her trance took her back behind her eyes and through the darkness until she was able to see herself clearly standing in nature. The gray pallor had completely left the landscape; young seedlings poked up through the ground. Finding her way to the massive World Tree, she searched for the opening into the trunk. She traveled down the roots until she came out into another place of nature. Looking around, she saw the two wells on either side of the tree roots and new growth around her. Finding a comfortable place near the Well of Forgetfulness, she laid on her back to surrender and called for the Bird Mother. Anne did not have long to wait long. Air moved about her; feathers touched her face. The Bird Mother had her in her talons! She wrenched the flesh from Anne's bones, picking them clean. There was no pain! When the Bird Mother was quite finished, she carried small pieces of Anne's body to the headsman, who pulverized her and tossed the remains into the fire.

Released of the two things she feared the most, Anne watched the flames about her. She then saw herself as the fire. When nothing was left but ash, the Bone Goddess gathered Anne's bones and placed them into a caldron. In a short time, Anne rose out of the caldron looking somewhat different. Unburdened, she surrendered her fate.

On the way back to the World Tree, Snake appeared. Anne was grateful that he had not abandoned her for good. When they reached the Tree, Snake hissed loudly, "Drink from the Well of Remembrance before going up the roots."

As she traveled up the roots, Anne felt the energies of earth and water, the elements of the Goddess, rising with her. Instead of ending her journey by traveling out the hole in the trunk, Anne continued on into the limbs of the Tree. Soft, fragrant leaves brushed against her cheek. Rising higher still, energies of air and fire, the elements of God, nudged her on. Up into the night sky and higher still, she felt as if she were riding on a beam of light towards a shining star. Arriving in the Upperworld, she found herself in a beautiful place in nature. Grandmother appeared, looking just as Anne remembered her. Then grandmother began to get younger; her form changed into an angelic-like creature of great beauty. When Anne gasped, grandmother assumed her familiar form.

"Anne, I think that this will be more comfortable for you as we travel together!" Anne smiled and Grandmother continued! "We have been waiting for you. Allow me to take you on a short tour of the Upperworld." Grandmother showed Anne places of healing where mercy might be found. Angels sang in vibrant, multiple harmonics. Coming to a lake shimmering of purity, Grandmother spoke, "Anyone who is able to reach these shores, may paint their hearts desire."

When she returned down through the branches and out the hole in the trunk, Anne remembered what had happened in the Underworld and traveling to the Upperworld. She was, however, unable to recall what happened at the jewel-like lake. What had she painted - if anything? Frustrating! Coming back to full consciousness, Anne looked down at her hands; they had stopped trembling. Feeling better than she had for a long time, she sent for Cramner that he might hear her confession. Shortly afterwards, Henry arrived at York, surprising Anne by offering comfort and apologized for ignoring her. Then he made sweet love to her.

INSTRUCTOR: It is said that when the World Tree returns to Mother Earth, the world will be made green and whole again. By working with the World Tree in the Otherworlds, you are helping to bring it back to Earth. When you are willing to release and heal fears and other issues, you help yourself, and Mother Earth as well. When I begin beating the drum you will see yourself clearly in your mind's eye standing in a beautiful place in nature. Go to the World Tree and call for the Mother Bird.

EXPERIENCE OF LENA LIDMALM OF SWEDEN: I sat in the tree. The Mother Bird came and sat on my shoulders, but she did not tear the flesh off of my body. I did feel a hard pressure in my heart.

INSTRUCTOR: Is there still pressure?

LENA: Yes!

INSTRUCTOR: I'll place my hands on your chest. By an act of will, push the heaviness into my hands. Good! Take a deep breath and exhale as I pull this off of you. Good! I'll put my hands back on your chest. Breathe in love; fill your heart with compassion.

EXPERIENCE OF ANGELA JOHANSSON OF SWEDEN: I saw a big eagle with a white head. She took my flesh away. When she was finished she put me into the fire. I came out a young woman who was taller than I am.

EXPERIENCE OF ANDREAS BLOMBERG OF SWEDEN: The Mother Bird took me up to a cliff to some hungry baby birds. She was going to drop me down to them but I said, "No!" So, she took me to the cauldron but an airplane came and took me up in a net. We went into space and looked at the moon.

EXPERIENCE OF HANNI BLOMBERG OF SWEDEN: The Mother Bird was a big vulture. She took me like a rag doll and tore the flesh off my body and threw it to a large hairy spider. Then the Mother Bird took my skeleton to the cauldron. I waited and waited. My guide told me, "You are not coming back. You are coming with me!" I found myself looking down at the cauldron — it was empty and I was standing next to my guide.

EXPERIENCE OF WILLEM BOEREN OF THE NETHERLANDS: The Mother Bird came as you said. She tore me apart and swallowed me. I wondered why I didn't die. She answered my thoughts, "This is about you completely surrendering."

She spit me out. Ants came and chewed what remained off my bones. The Bird picked up my bones and threw me into a very hot cauldron. It felt good!

I got my body back and ended up under the tree. The Mother Bird came to me and asked, "Are you reborn?"

"I think so!"

"Show me!"

I put my hands on her to give her a healing. She said, "The next time you want to heal yourself, come to me and I'll eat you again."

EXPERIENCE OF MARIAN VALKENBURGH OF THE NETHERLANDS: I went to the tree and the Bird took the anger from my liver, the sorrow of my heart and fear in my stomach. Then she pecked me apart. She took me to a cauldron with fire in it. When she put me in, the cauldron felt strangely empty.

The cauldron began to fill. It felt strange, but nice. As I was getting my body back, I realized that I was bigger than before. I felt much better, however, there is still an uncomfortable feeling in my liver. I think that I have to go back to the Mother Bird again.

EXPERIENCE OF JOAO RAMOS OF PORTUGAL: I went to the World Tree. The Mother Bird came and took me away. She took me apart in pieces, which she gave to animals to eat. I felt bad.

She put my bones in a cauldron. I grew again. I opened my eyes. She put white clothes on me. I sat comfortably listening to the drum.

EXPERIENCE OF ANDRE BEUKERS OF THE NETHERLANDS: I was sitting and waiting for the Mother Bird under the World Tree. Instead, an angel came and took me to the Queen's Chamber in the Great Pyramid. The angel told me that I had done enough and that I needed to rest.

There was a chair and I sat down and meditated. I felt refreshed. I feel very good now!

SEVEN RAYS INITIATION: One of the original books on the seven rays discusses these rays in terms of 7 colors (red, orange, yellow, green, blue, indigo and violet) and the corresponding personality traits of each of the rays. There are books on color therapy. There is a chapter in Reiki & Other Rays of Touch Healing giving suggestions on how to use colors in healing. The seven rays initiation given in the Shamanic I class balances the 7 directions in the heart and opens the gem-like chakras in the fingertips. It might be considered a Shamanic initiation of sorts because the Shaman works with the 7 directions.

Shamanic initiations given in both indigenous societies and inductions into magical rites in ancient Egypt are not passed down from an initiator to a student. Rather, Shamanic initiations come after long periods of study and practice, during which the Shaman becomes proficient in her/his craft and conquers all fears. These initiations consisted of walking through rattlesnake pits, or swimming the crocodile-infested Nile River. The culminating initiation in Egypt was the 72-hour initiation, during which the initiate lay in high meditation in a sealed casket. The Dead Sea Scrolls tell of how Jesus went through this initiation in Egypt, where he lived with his parents after they left Bethlehem. The following is from Reiki & Other Rays of Touch Healing:

Lazarus may be the last known man on earth to go through the three-day initiation of sustained high meditation described earlier. Lazarus' sisters had sent for Jesus so that he might bring their brother back from 'the land of the dead'. Yet, when Jesus arrived, he was told that he was too late; 'Lazarus is dead'. Lazarus had been unable to sustain and then break the state of suspended animation by himself; thus, his physical body perished. Jesus then performed his second greatest miracle, raising Lazarus' dead body. Later, Jesus would perform the ultimate miracle - laying down his own body and resurrecting it back to life."

It is also mentioned in the New Testament that Jesus taught his Disciples how to heal. Furthermore, he sent them out to heal and to teach others how to heal. They did not have to spend the night in a den of lions to become healers. Rather, the initiations Jesus gave his followers allowed them to heal, and opened the door for self-healing and examination. The 7 rays initiation, as well as the other initiations given in this class, are Universal attunements, which open psychic and healing abilities. It is also a requirement that the healer heal her/himself. To accomplish this, a sacrifice of the personal is required. In this case, the sacrifice is to scrutinize, relinquish and heal destructive habits, and detrimental emotional and mental patterns.

SEVEN RAYS INITIATION:

EXPERIENCES OF MARY K HAYDEN OF IRELAND: I felt this huge heat and power. There was tingling up from my elbow, across my shoulders and to the other elbow. My fingertips tingled as well. My heart feels expanded. Interestingly, my toes and feet are also tingling.

EXPERIENCE OF TRUDY VAN DER JAGT OF THE NETHERLANDS: The initiation was like rain coming down. I still feel tingling energy in my fingertips.

EXPERIENCES OF PATRICIA ROSEBOOM OF THE NETHERLANDS: I felt like a blanket was coming down around me. I also feel the tingling.

EXPERIENCE OF JOAO RAMOS OF PORTUGAL: I still feel the energy in my fingers. There was a pressure in my head. There is still cold coming down.

INSTRUCTOR: Is there still pressure in your head?

JOAO RAMOS: No!

INSTRUCTOR: Sometimes, uncomfortable sensations come up during a journey or initiation. These pains are coming up to be released. If the pain persists after the journey or initiation, please tell me so that I can pull it off.

EXPERIENCES OF DONNIE HUNTER OF GEORGIA: I felt the energy come down in bolts.

EXPERIENCES OF RYAN ALLEN NEAL OF FLORIDA: When I closed my eyes I saw six lights above me, and a nice aura around me.

EXPERIENCES OF DOMINIKA KULIGOWSKA OF POLAND: I felt a punch in my heart and my fingertips felt swollen. I can still feel it.

Middleworld

The Middleworld might be described as the astral body of Mother Earth. When somebody astral travels out of their body, they travel between the world of flesh and spirit. When a Shaman journeys inward to the Middleworld, this is where s/he is able to facilitate healings for Mother Earth, and ascertain knowledge.

In the following journeys to the Middleworld to heal Mother Earth, the students were asked to take along the symbol that is in the chapter on creativity, *How Are We To Color Outside the Lines When We Can't Locate the Crayons?* This symbol releases the cause of self-destructive behavior by liberating the memory that causes negative patterns to repeat. At that point the memory might be healed. Specifically, the students were asked to find the initial memory or core issue behind greed and corruption on Earth.

INSTRUCTOR: When I begin beating the drum you will see yourself clearly in your mind's eye in a beautiful place in nature. You will ask the power animals, nature spirits, angels and other spirit helpers to join you. This is your mission should you choose to accept it: Ask to be taken to a place that is on, in or above Mother Earth that requires healing. Do NOT decide where it is you are going. Allow the Spirit Helpers to take you to where you might do the most good at this time. When you get to your destination, ask your guides what to do. Keep asking questions. If something is taken off remember that the void needs to be filled. Ask your guides what to do.

EXPERIENCES OF VICKIE EBERLEIN OF GEORGIA: I met a group of animals and we traveled with the symbol to different places to heal Mother Earth.

EXPERIENCES OF DONNIE HUNTER OF GEORGIA: The healing went through a representative of the inner child of the collective consciousness. I was told that some of the greatest wisdom comes from the inner child, who sees things in a simple way, without ego.

EXPERIENCES OF RYAN ALLEN NEAL OF FLORIDA: Owl met me! I watched myself meditating about the greed and corruption on earth. Then it became just the opposite, I felt compassion.

EXPERIENCES OF DOMINIKA KULIGOWSKA OF POLAND: There was a group of people sitting and looking at something. I realized that they were looking at their own thoughts. Some of them were beautiful and others were dark and ugly. The angels meditated on the dark pictures and change them.

EXPERIENCES OF ANTHONY TORRES OF GEORGIA: I fell but I landed on my feet. I wore boots and pants, but no shirt, and I had a shovel tied to my back. The symbol was golden, and I carried it in a bag tied to my belt. I took the shovel and started digging, but these horrible little creatures kept trying to stop me. I identified them as corruption and greed. When I felt that it was time to stop digging, I sat down and took the golden symbol out. I meditated with the symbol and could feel its vibration. I don't know why this keeps happening to me, but the symbol began turning in a speed beyond description. It turned into light. The symbol and myself enter the earth as light. I sat in the earth like that for a very long, long time. When I came back out of the hole, everything around me was so bright. The horrible creatures were completely gone. I filled the hole up and came back.

JEANIE WARE OF GEORGIA: I was in a jungle at the base of a pyramid when we started off. I found an opening into the pyramid. It was completely dark. I asked for the symbol, angels, power animals and spirit guides to help heal the earth. A beam of light appeared. I found myself above the Earth looking down at pockets of corruption and greed. The angels wanted to isolate these pockets of corruption so that other people would be free to institute changes. Angels placed domes over political corruption in China, the United States, England and the Middle East, encapsulating dishonest individuals so that they became transparent and could do no more harm. Then the angels cut black tentacles between these countries, isolating corrupt elements from one another. People who hid under shrouds were now exposed.

NANCY MOORE OF NORTH CAROLINA: I started off in an open field with the animals. This time, I went down into the Otherworlds on a slide. I came out into an open field and asked for the symbol, and angels and other powerful beings who could help heal Mother Earth. We began with the water. There is too much warm water in the oceans. I watched as new ice was formed at the Poles. We also worked to release negative energy and calm the Earth down.

The power animals told me that too many people in positions of power do not care about the Earth or her inhabitants. I watched as the power animals removed these individuals from places of authority. The power animals empowered people who did not think that they had a voice. They gave these individuals the strength and the position from which to be heard.

SHAMANIC II: In the Shamanic II class the students are asked to go into the Middleworld as the Celts journeyed by finding the World Tree.

INSTRUCTOR: When I begin beating the drum you will see yourself clearly in your mind's eye standing in a beautiful place in nature. Look for the World Tree and ask to be taken to the Middleworld. Call upon your power animals, spirit helpers and angels to assist and help you facilitate a healing for Mother Earth. Remember to keep asking questions — Where do I go? What do I do? Is there anything else to do?

EXPERIENCE OF LENA LIDMALM OF SWEDEN: I called for my power animals. I waited! At last the owl came. Owl told me, "It is very bad in the earth and atmosphere. It is the reason why at this time, there are many natural disaster of great magnitude."

I suddenly became huge and took Mother Earth into my hands. She became like a crystal. Everything turned pink and then violet. Then I saw a butterfly.

EXPERIENCE OF ANGELA JOHANSSON OF SWEDEN: I saw a beautiful woman. She told me that I must help my closest friend. We went to a wetland that smelled really bad. I was asked to take away the odor.

EXPERIENCE OF ANDREAS BLOMBERG OF SWEDEN: I called for my power animals and was surprised when an alligator came. We don't have them in Sweden. Alligator said that the surface was very bad; there was a lot of pollution. We had a long discussion about it. Then we talked about the possibility of airbags for people traveling in airplanes and an airbag under airplanes. As we talked of these things, we seemed to be putting thoughts into the ethers.

EXPERIENCE OF HANNI BLOMBERG OF SWEDEN: I asked for my guides and a dolphin came. She was upset that the water was so dirty. I asked, "What can I do?"
The dolphin said, "People must understand that they cannot throw just anything into the water."
The dolphin left and a man with a dark complexion came. He said that he worked for Mother Earth. He told me that the dead must be burned. He also said that people are taking and taking, and not giving back to the Earth. Together we sent healing to Mother Earth.

EXPERIENCE OF ANDRE BEUKERS OF THE NETHERLANDS: I went down the tree. When I came out there was a large group of animals — lions, horses and many others. They all had baskets of roses. A monkey emptied his basket over me. We started walking. Each animal in turn gave me his basket. As I strew the roses, they cleared the Earth.

I came to a mountain where I found a book, but the pages were empty. In each page I was directed to place a rose.

INSTRUCTOR: The book with the empty pages represented Earth's future. By diligently placing a rose in each and every page, Andre was helping to insure Earth's future.

WILLEM BOEREN OF THE NETHERLANDS: My power animals, Grey Wolf and Bald Eagle (who is very big), guided me in my quest into the Underground. The Underground had not changed; it was still a beautiful place in nature. I found a pyramid and entered it with my power animals. When we reached an opening, Grey Wolf and Bald Eagle stood guard as I proceeded down a flight of stairs. I finally reached a level where there were no doors, only a plain, wooden hatch, which was partially covered with sand. I opened the hatch to find myself in a large room that seemed to go on forever. A big, golden Buddha statue with a great ruby at his 3rd eye stood amidst a treasure so big that the whole world could benefit from it. The statue spoke to me, saying that he and a woman (whom I could not see) were the keepers of the treasure. The rubies, emeralds, gold, etc. would be given to people in such a way that it would be available to all who were seeking.

Mathematically, the possible number of planets with intelligent life is in the millions. However, when the point of technology is reached when intelligent life is able to destroy itself, the number of probable planet with intelligent life drops to ten. As expeditions are launched to Mars, we may discover the last remnants of a war-like civilization in the structure that has the carved face of a human head on it, and the large surrounding geometric structures that are algebraically in relationship to one another. Accidental anomaly when Mars was formed? Hardly!

There is an asteroid belt between Mars and Jupiter, which holds enough material to form a planet. What if this planet really existed until the residents blew themselves up? The asteroid that hit Earth and eventually formed what we know now as our Moon may well have been a chunk from this planet.

Every time a Shaman heals her/himself or the planet, the probability of Earth going more easily into the Golden Age of the Return of the Angels increases. Besides the journeywork described above, there are additional methods that the Shaman may use for healing. These include, sending lost souls to the Light, clearings, and vortex healing.

SENDING LOST SOULS TO THE LIGHT: The Shaman has the ability to form a circle of energy around her/him. When the Shaman calls in the energy *(Chapter 2)*, spirits and angels step into the circle — it is called holding ceremony. The elemental healing energy the Shaman channels allows healings to occur for human members who have gathered in the circle for ceremony.

The Shaman may use these same abilities to ask the angels to open the vortex of light, which souls of the departed travel in to the Upperworlds or heaven. The angels use the healing energy that the Shaman is channeling to heal earthbound souls before they step into the light. After the earthbound souls have gone to the light with the angels, any demons who would like to make a transition into the light are invited to take the hand of an angel and go to the light. Lastly, if the Shaman is without fear and is channeling sufficient healing energy, s/he invites the angels to bring any black magic into the circle for transformation.

Typically, there is a lot of black magic brought into the circle by the angels for transmutation! It is surprising how many people use it to attain positions of power and wealth, seemingly unaware that there are consequences. Or perhaps, it is because they think that penalties are for everyone else, not them! Books are sold on how to do black magic spells and call in demons. It is quite easy to do, which is why it is called the easy way. The black magician stands in the middle of a pentagram — not because the pentagram is evil but because it is a symbol of protection. However, (and this is a rather big "however") there is only so much a symbol can do. From the first time a demon is summoned, it forms an attachment to the black magician that is carried to the grave. There are many people who have taken the easy way rather than the right way. The *Harry Potter* books deal with the clash between good and evil, and the costs of evil. Interestingly enough, black magicians ardently and openly denounce any kind of magic because they do not want people using white magic to break their spells. In the *Harry Potter* books one the goals of Voldamort and his followers is to close Hogwarts. It is without doubt that

J. K. Rawlings receives a great deal of information and support from higher beings and celestial angels.

Some people make blanket statements that healing and magic are evil, even though Jesus performed magic when he turned water into wine and walked on water. A blanket statement by its very definition has to include everybody, even Jesus — he sets the example! Unconditional declarations are fixed without exception! When religious leaders make absolute statements and followers are expected to adhere to these decisions without questioning, they are using brainwashing techniques, as described in pages 11 - 14.

The best way to teach or set standards is by example. If a leader does or does not do something, subordinates take this into consideration when they make their choices. It is the way in which God helps us learn our lessons. God offers us free will choice. In my college sociology class on Deviant Social Behavior, the instructor made one statement that has remained in my conscious mind. That is, people ought to be allowed to do whatever they want to, except when their actions interfere with the rights of others.

WHAT TO KEEP IN MIND WHEN DOING CLEARINGS: There are things to remember when releasing demons to the Light for forgiveness, or black magic to the Light or Violet Fire for transformation. The first is for everyone to stay out of judgment with those who perform black magic. Judgment draws those who judge into the game, and this is one game that the wise refrain from entering. The second is for the Shaman to ask the angels to set up diversionary tactics so that the black magicians cannot discover who has unraveled their spells. The third is to cloak everyone in the circle with silver, the color of invisibility. The fourth is to fill in the voids that are left with love, compassion and forgiveness. If justice is asked for, it is prudent to ask for God's mercy and grace as well. In this way, when justice is meted out to those who request it for others, God's mercy and grace will also be there.

The following is from the chapter, *Canterbury Tales,* in *Part II* of <u>Between Two Worlds: The Story of Henry VIII and Anne Boleyn — and Her Celtic Heritage</u>:

Saint Peter's Church in Kent, England is close to Hever Castle and was built by William de Hevre in the 13th century, over the site of an earlier Norman church. The main part of the church was built in the mid 14th century; Geoffrey Boleyn built the Boleyn Chapel in 1465. Changing architectural styles may be observed in both the pillars and windows. The remains of Thomas Boleyn, who died in 1538, two years after the deaths of George and Anne, lay in a tomb in the Boleyn Chapel. Beside his tomb are buried the remains of his infant son, Henry. After the execution of two of his three children, Thomas Boleyn left court a broken man. Thomas Boleyn's lands and titles in Ireland were taken away from him. Under ordinary circumstances, Hever Castle would have been taken away as well, but Henry

VIII allowed Elizabeth and Thomas to live at Hever so long as they lived.

The deeper the expressed or suppressed negative emotion, the more narrowly defined are the parameters within which an earthbound spirit may move about. It is as if the burden of negativity constricts the very vibration of the soul. An individual during his or her life authors the purgatory or heaven that he or she lives in after death. Hell is not God's doing, it is our own creation. Thomas Boleyn died with a millstone of guilt, regret, sorrow and shame firmly affixed like armor under his shroud. Neville read in the church's brochure, *St. Peter's Church Hever, Kent,* "On the tomb is one of the finest monumental brasses in the country. It shows the full robes and insignia of a Knight of the Garter with the badge on the left breast and the Garter round the left knee. A falcon, the crest of the family, is above the right shoulder and at the feet is a griffin."

Turning around to take a closer look at the sepulcher, I was completely taken aback. The inside of the tomb was visible. The colors of the body, the clothes and the crypt were nasty shades of dark, murky browns and yellows. Lying both over and through the corpse was the spirit of Thomas Boleyn. Elizabeth had died just months prior to her husband's death. Looking at Thomas Boleyn in his misery, it was clear that he had pressured Anne and manipulated events so that she would marry Henry. An

inner knowing came like a thunderbolt;
Lily was a reincarnation of George
Boleyn.

"What to do?"

"Speak to Thomas Boleyn as
though you were Anne. Tell him that he
is forgiven. It is time for him to
forgive himself and go to the Light."

Thomas Boleyn turned slowly to
look at me. I did as the angels
requested. Thomas seemed relieved.
Asking the angels to open the vortex,
I held my hands up to send healing and
repeated the prayer: "You are loved,
blessed, healed and forgiven! You are
loved, blessed, healed and forgiven!
You are loved, blessed, healed and
forgiven! You are one with your own
higher self! Take the hand of an
angel! Go to the Light. Go with
Jesus, go with Mary, go with Buddha,
go with Quan Yen! Go now! Go with
angels, go with the Great White
Brotherhood, go with the Saints, go
with the Bodhisattvas! Go now! Go to
heaven, go to the Light! Go now! Go to
peace, mercy, light, love, joy,
enlightenment! Go now!" After
repeating the prayer two more times,
Thomas Boleyn was released from his
earthly bounds and left in the vortex
of Light with the angels. Neville held
out his hands as well. Healing energy
flowed through us, filling the void of
Thomas' passage with love. The church
itself seemed to breathe a sigh of
relief.

EXPERIENCE OF LENA LIDMALM OF SWEDEN:
I didn't see anyone step into the middle of
our circle and go to the Light. However, I

162

felt the heaviness in the room of those who had come. My hands were heavy from their energy. After a while the heaviness left the room and my hands.

INSTRUCTOR: By asking for only those who are ready to make a transition into the Light, we have set the parameters or guidelines of who exactly is invited to come into the room. As with other healings, if you feel your hands getting heavy, take one hand and work it down the other arm starting at the elbow. Pull the heaviness down to the fingertips and out. Send the weight down to the central fire for transformation or to the Light for purification.

EXPERIENCE OF ANGELA JOHANSSON OF SWEDEN: I could see lots of people come into the circle. It was very heavy. I could feel healing energy in my hands and feet. I saw the Light and felt a lot of love.

EXPERIENCE OF ANDREAS BLOMBERG OF SWEDEN: For the most part I didn't feel anything. For only a short time, I felt something in my hands but I didn't recognize it.

EXPERIENCE OF HANNI BLOMBERG OF SWEDEN: There was a lot of energy in my hands. I could not see the souls who came except for one little girl. With the demons, I felt a tightness in my throat and that the energy was very heavy. There was lots of heat.

EXPERIENCES OF DONNIE HUNTER OF GEORGIA: At one point, with my physical eyes I saw a little demon step into the

163

Light. My fingers are pulsating with energy, like my palms usually do when I am doing healings. I have never experienced this before.

Under circumstances whereby any of the circle's participants are left with any heaviness or misgivings whatsoever, the Hosanna Clearing is a good way to clear the room and everyone in it. To learn the Hosanna Clearing, the following is another quote from the chapter, *Canterbury Tales,* in *Part II* of <u>Between Two Worlds: The Story of Henry VIII and Anne Boleyn — and Her Celtic Heritage</u>:

Brenda felt the energy just around Anne's bedroom required clearing, but there were other tourists in the building. However, it felt as if the angels were in strong agreement with Brenda. So, while Brenda closed her eyes and held her hands out to lend her energy to the project, I began drawing the Hosanna symbols and energizing them. Most of the people that walked by had no idea whatsoever what was going on. There were a few people who knew that something was up. One or two actually felt the energy transformation. So as not to unduly disturb anyone, I tried as best I could to invoke the incantation when people were not about.

"Saint Michael the Archangel, Saint Michael the Archangel, Saint Michael the Archangel! Your legions of helpers, your legions of angels! By your flaming swords, jaws, talons and claws cut and release any ties any cords other than God's desire that are in, through, round and about, above, below, within and without this room." The dark energy broke. I drew more Hosanna symbols. "Angels of the Violet Fire, Angels of the Violet Fire, Angels of the Violet Fire! Take any psychic debris that Michael and his legions are cutting free by their flaming swords, jaws, talons and claws. Release, release to the Violet Fire! Transform, transform by Violet Fire! Consume, consume by Violet Fire! Transmute, transmute by Violet Fire!" After repeating the chant to the Angels of the Violet Fire, negative energy altered to a higher vibration. The angels took what remained away! As the Universe does not like a void, it is best to ask the angels to fill the space with positive energy rather than throw the dice, walk away and take a chance on what comes in. "Celestial angels, Christed beings, Buddhas, fill in the voids with healing, love, forgiveness, mercy, grace, enlightenment, truth." The shift was notable!

The Middleworld may also be accessed directly through nature. There are stories of people lying down on the earth or sand and becoming aware of the heartbeat of Mother Earth. As the vibration came into them, they were healed. There are stories of people encountering nature spirits and receiving gifts, information or healing. Here is a short excerpt from the chapter *The Bronte Family — All of Them!* From *Part II* of <u>Between Two Worlds</u>:

Nearly ten years later, Brenda Davies and I went to Howath, England — Bronte country. Emily Bronte had written *Wuthering Heights* and Charlotte Bronte was the author of *Jane Eyre.* After learning that a third sister, Anne, had written *Agnes Grey* and *The Tenant of Wildfel Hall,* there was a persistent thought that this was too much of a coincidence. Rather than being born with this gift, this gift had come in another way, a spiritual way, to the three girls.

The land, the moors and the town are very much as they had been in the mid 1800's. The English love to hike and there are paths that people come to walk in undisturbed nature. It is in the wild areas, where development and cement have not blotted out the landscape, that nature spirits may be found. The pamphlets all stated that the Bronte girls played fantasy games outdoors with fairies. That's where they had gotten their gift of writing!

THE SPIRIT OF THE MOUNTAIN: Hanni and Andreas live on the side of a mountain. Their home is typical of what most Americans think modern Swedish homes look like. It is open and spacious with wooden floors, large glass windows and doors. There is even a sauna on the ground floor. The road in the back of their home leads to a nature preserve. The preserve is visible from their backyard, where moose and deer frequently graze on grass, shrubbery and flowers in the evening hours.

Serenity in the preserve is not quite what it should be. Motorcycles and motorbikes careen the woodland paths, even though they are not officially allowed. There is also a relatively new golf course in the preserve.

The ideal time to go would have been early in the morning, before the sun rose over the horizon. The in-between time offers a greater chance of encountering Otherworld beings and phenomenon. Messages may be heard on the wind, as it picks up in the early hours of the day.

Our group found its way to the small lake. Each one lay down upon the earth and flat stone trying to feel the heartbeat of Mother Earth. Outside noises were used to go more deeply within. Afterwards, to everyone's surprise, everyone had had some experience of someone walking around. However, when we had opened our eyes to see who was there, there was no one.

After leaving the lakeshore, the group stopped at a place where only the year before, Hanni and I had sent lost souls to the Light. The place was calmer and somehow more alive. Everyone stood with her/his back to a tree, attempting to feel nature and the presence of the spirit of the mountain. Hanni was the first to see the gnarled, hooded old man — the spirit of the mountain. He confirmed that he was displeased with the motorcycles, motorbikes and new golf course. Then he asked us to send healing to the woods and the mountain, which he protected. During the healing a golden light appeared. Each one in our group received a blessing.

HOOGALOON: Fairies and the spirits of nature are so much a part of the history and culture of Hoogaloon in southern Holland that a public statue of a gnome was commissioned and placed in the town. Many stories are told of these beings. More often than not, gnomes lay hidden outside the range of ordinary vision. However, in Hoogaloon they make frequent appearances.

Local residents organize regular walking tours. Guides and visitors meander the tree-lined lanes or ride in carriages. Sites where gnomes have been spotted are meticulously pointed out to the believers and disbelievers.

What is for certain is that nature in Hoogaloon is more abundant than in other parts of Holland or Europe. Farmers leave large groves of trees between their fields, choosing not to flatten everything in sight. Larger wooded areas are public domain. Whenever humans make a conscious effort to preserve and honor nature, nature returns the favor and blesses the local farmers and residents.

Guided by local residents, we were taken to a place in an open field where they said three lay lines came together. They thought there might be an energy vortex where the lines crossed. There wasn't! Wherever there is an energy vortex, one will find a huge granite stone directly under the ground. New York City is like one large energy vortex because the city is built on the top of a flat granite mountain. Because its foundation is granite, New York City is able to hold many large buildings. Other islands might sink under such a weight.

Earth's rivers are likened to blood vessels and arteries; her lay lines might be thought of as her nervous system. Vortexes are similar to chakras or areas of concentrated energy that allow Earth to pull in and expel energy; it is as if the

Earth breathes through these portals. In doing a clearing and sending healing through the three lay lines in Hoogaloon, the healing was carried through the lay lines to energy vortexes.

After the healing we went in search of gnomes. We did not have far to look. In a nearby cluster of trees we each picked a tree and sat or stood with our spines against the tree trunk. The specific exercise was to allow the back chakras to one at a time go into the tree trunk for cleansing. As trees transform carbon dioxide into oxygen on a physical level, on an etheric level they take our negativity and transmute it into clean energy. Before long the gnomes came to work on each one of us. Some people saw them with their physical eyes and others with their 3rd eye. However, everyone felt the gnomes working on their aches and pains, diseases and issues. The relief was comforting and the healings real. So much so, that we stayed with our backs against the trees for over two hours.

VORTEX HEALING: The vortexes on Earth hold more energy than other places. Sedona, Arizona is one such place where there are many powerful vortexes. Here you will find tree trunks that have grown twisted in the energy. The closer to the energy, the more twisted the trunks and branches will be.

People come to vortexes to be healed — and that is one form of vortex healing. The Roman Catholic Church built its cathedrals and monasteries over sites where Shaman preformed rituals. Unsurprisingly, many of these sites were vortexes. I painted the cover of Tera, My Journey Home: Alternative Healing at Holy Hill in Wisconsin, where many healings were performed before the Catholic Church put a stop to healings by the clergy.

The problem is that these energy vortexes can become polluted with human negative energy. To clear the vortexes, a Shaman may journey. However, many of these sites require a group effort as the buildup of toxicity has many deep layers. So, the group effort may consist of one person beating the drum while everyone else journeys to the same place.

To do the clearing in another way, the group stands around the vortex in a circle (although a circle is not always possible in rough natural terrain). Angels, power animals, spirit guides are called to come in and help. This may be done in the elaborate Native American 20 Count or simply by calling in several powerful ascended beings and archangels. Each person builds Universal healing energy in the circle by repeatedly feeling the energy come into her/his crown and sending it onto the person on her/his right, and receiving energy from the person on her/his left. When the energy has been sufficiently built up, it is given to God through the angels and spirit guides who have come to help with the clearing. They are asked to multiply the healing energy again and to send it into the Earth. In a meditative state, each member of the group watches the energy to see what is happening. To clear the negativity, everyone holds out their arms and hands straight in front of them. Everyone visualizes her/his arms and hands as powerful electromagnets, and then lifts the negativity to the Light for purification and transformation. Then Light is brought into fill in the voids.

Healing Power of Color, Nature & the Ascended Masters

In Shamanic I students are connected to the colors, a place in nature where the color maybe found and to an ascended being. If the teacher is connected then s/he is able to help the students to connect. The benefit to having a deeper bond is that colors and nature are tools the Shaman uses. To have higher beings assist a Shaman is without question valuable. Many students find this to be the most powerful exercise in the class.

INSTRUCTOR: We will do one color at a time. I will give you the name of the color, where you are going and whom you will be meeting. After the drumming I will give you a place on your body to focus and some time to integrate the energy.

Cobalt blue: When I begin beating the drum you will see yourself clearly in your mind's eye standing in a beautiful place in nature. You will travel to the cobalt blue heart of Mother Earth. You will connect with Mother Earth's heart, the color cobalt blue and Hava, the mother of all living.
WHEN THE DRUMMING STOPS: Come back into your body. Bring back the color cobalt blue, your connection to the heart of Mother Earth, and with Hava. Pull the

171

cobalt blue into the soles of your feet and into your root chakra. Integrate the color cobalt blue!

Emerald Green: When I begin beating the drum you will see yourself clearly in your mind's eye standing in a beautiful place in nature. You will travel to the leaf of a tree, plant or herb. You will become very small so that you might explore this leaf. You will connect with the plant kingdom, the color emerald green and Barachiel, Pan and El Shaddai.

WHEN THE DRUMMING STOPS: Come back into your body. Bring back the color emerald green, your connection to the plant kingdom, and with Barachiel, Pan and El Shaddai. Pull the color emerald green into your front and back heart chakras. Integrate the color emerald green!

Indigo: When I begin beating the drum you will see yourself clearly in your mind's eye standing in a beautiful place in nature. You will travel to the western sky. The sun has just gone below the horizon. The first darkness of the evening sky is indigo (blue/purple). You will connect with the color indigo, Saint Lucy and Saint Martin, and the in-between time of dusk.

WHEN THE DRUMMING STOPS: Come back into your body. Bring back the indigo, your connection to the sunset, and with Saint Lucy and Saint Martin. Pull the color indigo into your third eye and the back of your head. Integrate the color indigo!

Violet: When I begin beating the drum you will see yourself clearly in your mind's eye standing in a beautiful place in

172

nature. You will travel to Mount Shasta. Find an opening into the mountain and connect with the Violet Flame, the color violet, and Saint Germain and Quan Yen.

WHEN THE DRUMMING STOPS: Come back into your body. Bring back the color violet, your connection to the mountains, and with Saint Germain and Quan Yen. Pull the color violet into your crown. Integrate the color violet!

Blue-green: When I begin beating the drum you will see yourself clearly in your mind's eye standing in a beautiful place in nature. You will travel to the sea. You will connect with the color blue-green, the sea, and with Neptune and Mira.

WHEN THE DRUMMING STOPS: Come back into your body. Bring back the color blue-green, your connection to the sea, and with Neptune and Mira. Pull the color blue-green into the soles of your feet and into your mouth. Taste the salt of the sea. Integrate the color blue-green!

Silver: When I begin beating the drum you will see yourself clearly in your mind's eye standing in a beautiful place in nature. You will travel to the moon. You will connect with the color silver, the moon and Isis and Mary.

WHEN THE DRUMMING STOPS: Come back into your body. Bring back the color silver, your connection to the moon, and with Isis and Mary. Feel the color silver in your aura. Integrate the color silver!

Pink: When I begin beating the drum you will see yourself clearly in your mind's eye standing in a beautiful place in nature. You will travel to the dawn. You will connect with the time in-between night and day, the color pink, and Archangel Gabriel and the Ascended Masters.

WHEN THE DRUMMING STOPS: Come back into your body. Bring back the color pink, your connection to the dawn, and with archangel Gabriel and the Ascended Masters. Pull the color pink into your front and back heart chakras. Integrate the color pink!

Orange: When I begin beating the drum you will see yourself clearly in your mind's eye standing in a beautiful place in nature. You will travel to the central core of lava within Mother Earth, or you may go into a volcano. You will connect with lava, the core of Earth, the color orange, and Buddha, Kahli and Babaji.

WHEN THE DRUMMING STOPS: Come back into your body. Bring back the color orange, your connection to Earth's core, and with Buddha, Kahli and Babaji. Pull orange into your front and back second chakras. Integrate the color orange!

Ruby Red: When I begin beating the drum you will see yourself clearly in your mind's eye standing in a beautiful place in nature. You will travel to the giant ruby, which the Atlantian emperors used to regenerate themselves. You may find yourself under the Atlantic Ocean, if so you will be able to breathe. The greater part of Atlantis is under miles of ice, a landmass we call Antarctica. You will find the Red ruby and connect to it, the color red and the energy of Christ Consciousness.

WHEN THE DRUMMING STOPS: Come back into your body. Bring back the color ruby red, your connection to the Atlantian ruby

174

and the gem and crystal kingdoms, and with the energy of Christ Consciousness. Pull the color into the soles of your feet, root and crown chakras. Integrate the color!

Yellow: When I begin beating the drum you will see yourself clearly in your mind's eye in a beautiful place in nature. You will travel to the sun. You will connect with the color yellow, the sun and Archangels Uriel, Metatron and Sandalphon.
WHEN THE DRUMMING STOPS: Come back into your body. Bring back the color yellow and gold, your connection to the sun, and with the Archangels. Pull the colors yellow and gold into your front and back solar plexus. Integrate the colors!

White: When I begin beating the drum you will see yourself clearly in your mind's eye standing in a beautiful place in nature. You will travel to the flower petal of a white rose, lily or apple blossom. You will become very small and explore this flower. You will connect with the flower, the color crystalline white and the Circle of Life or All There Is.
WHEN THE DRUMMING STOPS: Come back into your body. Bring back the color white and your connection to All There Is. Pull the color white into all of your chakras. Integrate the color white!

Black: Represents all lost knowledge and the Hidden Mystery, which is within us and draws us to the knowledge of the One. We cannot draw upon something that draws us; we can only bring it forth. Thus, to reach black, focus behind your eyes and keep going back. I will not beat the drum. Your silence will take you back. You may reach a point where it seems that you are standing on the edge of space. If you reach this point, step into it.

ONE WAY TO USE THE COLORS IN HEALING: The healee may meditate by focusing on the point behind his or her eyes, or the healee may see her/himself clearly in her/his mind's eye. The healer asks for the colors one at a time to be sent to the healee. The colors may be brought up one at a time through the sole of the right foot, up the leg, across the appropriate chakra and down the left side and out the left foot.

EXPERIENCES OF MARY K HAYDEN OF IRELAND: It was beautiful — I was surrounded and filled with cobalt blue. I could not see Hava, but I did see her blue cloak and the golden rays around her. She told me that Earth needed healing from the inside out. Healing is happening for Earth, and I was not to worry; just keep the healing going.

With indigo, it was Saint Martin and Saint Claire who welcomed me. Their message was to let go of the fear of seeing and knowing into the future. Enjoy the pictures into the future because I cannot do harm and I will not take advantage of people.

Mount Shasta was empty with the exception of the Violet color. St. Germaine said, "I am always with you."

Quan Yen asked me to use her name and call upon her. There were two ledges. On the first were warriors on dark brown horses. The warriors wore amulets and were dressed in deep violet and gold. Above them were hundreds of elephants going in the other direction from left to right.

I went down quickly and saw Neptune. The goddess of the sea said that my fear of the water was completely gone. If I went into the mode of a fish or bird with wings, lots more would be shown to me.

I became a little rosemary leaf growing. I was looking at the ants on the ground. They were busy chattering to one another. I liked that. I was in an organic garden and a person came. That person felt the stem, which I was on. It felt good.

When I went into the sun there was a huge golden glow and Jesus told me that he was there with me. His message was not to be afraid of being powerful. The guardian angels were all bowing. I was a bit uncomfortable and I asked them why they were doing that. They said, "Because we serve mankind."

I became part of the lava and moved with it. Lava is heat and fire and I was much more comfortable with it today than yesterday. I received great healing from it.

Strangely enough, to get to the ruby I went through a blade of grass and into the ground. I traveled all the way to the South Pole underground. I came up and found myself in this huge ice mountain. From there I ended up in a huge ruby. It was sending sparks, like stars, through me. I asked if there was anything I needed to know. I was told to stop delaying and go back to writing. With Christ Consciousness I felt that I was being blessed. There was great energy and healing from this energy.

Pink had a very calm peaceful feeling. I was filled and surrounded by the color and was healed by it. The ascended masters came to me as colors; there were no faces.

They said, "You need to ask us more often for help."

I was a giddy little thing, like a fairy, on a white daisy hopping from one petal to the next with abandoned joy. I was told that I needed to enjoy more. The daisy became the circle of life.

With black, I was surprised because I had no fear and was able to step off the edge. Black was peaceful and quite. Without the dark there would be no light.

EXPERIENCE OF DOROTHY OF NORTH CAROLINA, WHO DID NOT WISH TO HAVE HER REAL NAME USED: I entered through the top of the mountain and went deeper and deeper. I became the cobalt blue color and it became me. It is quite nice to be there.

As with each color, I went right to indigo and absorbed it. With each color, if a part of my body hurt, I sent the particular color we were working with to that part of my body. With each color, I became each color and it became me.

With green, I went from leaf to leaf to leaf of all of my favorite trees. I explored the leaves, as well as the different hues of each leaf. I was a little ant and very playful, which is very unlike me.

The energy of yellow was very powerful and I just glowed. It was the most powerful color that I experienced. I ran the yellow and gold both clockwise and counterclockwise into myself. I did the same with the orange.

To find the Atlantian ruby, I again went through the top of a mountain and ended up with ice above me. The deeper I went, the bigger the ruby became, and the more magnificent the shades of red appeared. I pulled the energy of Christ Consciousness up into me. It looped through me to the chakra above my crown, so that the energy ran in a tight oval.

I became lots of different flowers with different textures and hues of white. - orchid, apple blossom, rose and lilac. Then I became a fairy, who danced and kicked up her heals, which is very different from who I am. I said to myself, "Go girl!" The circle of life kept coming back. When it entered by body, it was very powerful, like the yellow or gold.

I kept going deeper and deeper into black. I wasn't fearful and I could feel myself teetering on the edge with it.

EXPERIENCE OF TRUDY OF THE NETHERLANDS: When I was in the sun with Metatron, Sandelphon and Uriel, my solar plexus felt huge. With green I felt the color. With blue-green I felt the energy at the back of my neck.

EXPERIENCE OF DENISE OF THE NETHERLANDS: With indigo I was dancing on the beach and I felt it strongly in my 3rd eye. The other color that left a strong impression was violet. I stood in a cave with amethyst all around me. It felt great!

EXPERIENCES OF PATRICIA OF THE NETHERLANDS: Saint Germain helped me with all of the colors. I met Buddha in the color orange and he embraced me.

EXPERIENCE OF JOAO RAMOS OF PORTUGAL: When seeing auras, I have only seen a few colors. Yesterday, I saw blue for the first time. Today, I saw green for the first time.

179

I had some difficulty finding the Atlantian ruby. With the color green I saw myself in a leaf playing. With violet there came a lot of energy into my hands.

EXPEIENCES OF FRANK OF THE NETHERLANDS: Orange went into my ears. With the color blue I felt air coming up my feet. The color green entered my heart.

EXPERIENCES OF VICKIE EBERLEIN OF GEORGIA: Today, I had trouble going to places by myself; I had to keep asking for help. The priestess, Aleeta, and priest, Dole, from yesterday kept showing up to give me support. To get to the red ruby, the Wicca broom from yesterday came to help me get there. I had to sweep away the ice with the broom.

The horse that took me into the Underworld yesterday, took me down today to the cobalt blue heart of Mother Earth. It was just so beautiful. Another color that I found particularly nice was the violet flame. I became the flame and danced in the flame with Quan Yen and Saint Germain and many other beings. I also danced inside of the orange. I laid down in the silver of the moon.

The yellow of the sun was the most powerful; it's funny, I have never liked yellow very much. Sandelphon and Metatron both appeared and I held their hands. I realized that if they could work themselves up from the pits of despair to archangel status, there was nothing that I could not do. It was wonderful!

EXPERIENCES OF DONNIE HUNTER OF GEORGIA: I guess that I will start out with green. It took me a minute to get inside of my leaf. The energy of the plant hit me on my right side. I felt as if I would fall out of this chair. When I went to the sun to see the two archangels that had fallen, they invited me into the fiery flame. I hesitated for a minute. Then I thought, "If they can do it, I can do it!" The energy was all around me. With silver it felt like somebody was standing behind me with her hands on my shoulders. It was quite nice! White was extremely peaceful — unimaginable peace! I could have floated in the black of the womb all day.

EXPERIENCES OF RYAN ALLEN NEAL OF FLORIDA: I found myself instantly surrounded by all of the colors except for black. I felt the absorption of the colors, and the colors flowing through my chakras. Black felt like serenity and floating.

EXPERIENCES OF DOMINIKA KULIGOWSKA OF POLAND: I liked the violet flame; it was very delicate and soft. When I was sitting in the flame, feathers surrounded me. When the fire or feathers touched me it felt nice. The other color I liked was red. I traveled to the Atlantian ruby through the ice. The vehicle I was in melted the ice. When I reached the giant ruby I sat in it; it was as big as a house. I felt really safe there. With white I found myself in a huge white lily. I could feel the petals and God's presence, and I could smell the aroma of the lily. It was nice!

EXPERIENCES OF ANTHONY TORRES OF GEORGIA: Every color had its own unique effect on me. I traveled at a gallop to Atlantis on the back of a lion. With each stride, he covered a mile. He told me to

181

hold onto his mane, and we went through South America. As we approached the polar area, the lion started growing more hair; his mane turned from tan-color to a white snow lion. When we reached the South Pole he jumped into the air, landed and started burrowing into the ice. He reached a certain point where he was unable to go further. He gave me his etheric paws with claws to use. I used them to dig through the ice. I made it! There were figures dressed in blue and white Egyptian garb. There was a moonstone colored light. I stepped up to the ruby, which was the size of a small building and protected by a glass globe. I climbed to the top of the globe and dropped down to the ruby. I sat down inside the ruby. I was surprised! Jesus came into the ruby and sat down across from me. He placed his left hand over my heart and his right hand on my shoulder. I did likewise to him. We were vibrating in this red space in meditation until it was time to come back.

In the blue a voice came to me and said, "I am the color of authority." Blue was a very solid color. The blue-green color was much lighter and wave-like. When I went to the lava, Babaji was waiting for me. It was not hot. The feeling was excitement and enthusiasm. It was very, very healing for me. The moon had lots and lots and lots of silver fairies. They showed me tricks that they do using the force and energy of the moon. They would go into the moon and come out of the moon and fly into the Earth's water with a great deal of momentum. They showed me how the moon works with the tides. Then I sat in meditation inside the silver.

Power Animal Retrieval

In infinite wisdom God created an interdependent world. Animals manage Mother Earth; they are part and parcel of eco systems. Sometimes, the benefits they bring are not readily observable. For example, hippos help to keep muddy rivers flowing. We discussed earlier how Earth is a living planet, as opposed to a lifeless planet. The animal kingdom and their roles in nature help to keep Earth alive.

The Native Americans have an expression; that is, when there are no more eagles Earth will die. Why? While hawks and falcons may be found in New York City, there are no eagles. Eagles survive in wilderness habitats. Desert or lava planets in science fiction literature and movies are improbable environments for advanced life. Without oxygen (plants turn carbon dioxide into oxygen) and clean water (eco systems keep water running and clean), higher life forms cannot exist.

Animals are in tune with nature. In India after the tsunami, it was discovered that many animals survived. These animals knew in advance that something big and dangerous was coming. They fled while many unsuspecting people meandered to the shore to see what was happening.

A Shaman looks to nature to find God. (God may be found in everything — that's in the Bible.) Shaman discovered cures in plants and listened to the messages of the wind. Early Shaman also observed that each animal brings a gift to humanity. This may have started when early man prayed to the spirits of the animals they hunted, requesting them to sacrifice members of the herd. An animal's gift to humanity is typically its outstanding characteristic. A ram has the energy of striking force and surefootedness, as does goat. Giraffe's long neck helps him to observe the whole situation. If a Shaman or another individual strongly exhibited the distinctiveness of a particular animal, s/he was said to carry the energy of that particular animal. Or it was said that the animal was a power animal of the Shaman or individual.

What are some of the other gifts that animals bring to humanity? Cats are psychic. For example, many house cats follow unseen apparitions or objects with their eyes. Butterfly, scarab and snake are animals whose outstanding characteristic is transformation. Coyote is the trickster; however, his deceptions oftentimes fail to work to his advantage. If an individual carries coyote medicine, by the folly of his acts we see our own shortcomings and self-sabotaging actions. Raven's energy in many cultures is magic. His black color represents the Womb of Creation or the Great Mystery. While deer is gentleness, stag's power is akin to Christ Consciousness — an awareness of the healing power within the Earth.

The Sphinx is the guardian of the animals and the animal kingdoms and the keeper of the secret of animal medicine. While each animal brings a specific gift, when the wilderness is destroyed and species become extinct, both the animal and their gift leave Earth. We lose our connection to animal gifts or powers through misuse or lack of use.

Animal medicine may be acquired or re-acquired through a Shamanic ceremony known as power animal retrieval. In this ceremony the Shaman lies down next to the healee and touches his shoulder to the shoulder of the healee. While someone beats the drum, the Shaman journeys into the Otherworlds to look for the healee's missing power animal. Traditionally, when the Shaman sees the same animal three times, it is the healee's missing power animal. The Shaman invites the animal into his hands and magically the animal shrinks in size if need be. The Shaman brings his etheric and physical hands to his heart chakra, which is at the sternum. The Shaman journeys back to the physical world, and then blows the missing power animal into the heart chakra and third eye of the healee. He takes a rattle and shakes it around the healee to ground the energy. In modern times, clapping the hands and clicking the fingers accomplishes the same objective.

If there are an odd number of students in the class, then someone is paired with the instructor. As the instructor is unable to both beat the drum and journey, her/his partner will have to beat the drum while the instructor journeys. Partners are changed in the next exercise, so someone else will be paired with the instructor.

INSTRUCTOR: You will find a partner - hopefully, somebody whom you do not know. You may always work with your friends after the class. Choose who is going to be the Shaman and who is going to be the healee. You will lie down next to one another or sit next to one another in such a way that your shoulders or knees touch one another. When I begin beating the drum, the healee

185

will stay here in meditation. Shaman, when I begin beating the drum you will see yourself clearly in your mind's eye standing in a beautiful place in nature. You will look for an opening into the Underworld. Travel into the Underworld and begin looking for your partner's missing power animal. The third time you see the same animal (or bird, etc.) it is the missing power animal. So you might see an eagle, a lizard, a bear, a buffalo, a lizard and another lizard. The lizard is the missing power animal. *(Stay out of judgment! The lizard is probably exactly what your partner needs.)* If you are in doubt that this is the missing power animal, then ask.

As the vibration of Earth is going up (and that is scientifically measurable), ceremonies and journeywork are becoming easier to do. For example, an animal may simply present himself to you and say that he is the missing power animal. You don't have to take his word. You may ask him to prove it. He won't be offended! When you have established which animal is the missing power animal you may ask him or her, "What gift do you bring for my partner?"

Hold out your etheric and your physical hands. The missing power animal will jump into your hands. Bring your etheric and physical hands back to your chest. Hold the Power Animal gently in your cupped hands. *(If you are bringing back an elephant, the elephant will automatically become small and fit into your hands.)* Come back the same way you went down. Place your cupped hands over the healee's heart and blow the missing power animal into your partner's heart.

Place your cupped hands over the third eye and blow the missing power animal into your partner's third eye. Traditionally, you rattle around the individual. Clapping your hands and clicking your fingers also works to ground the energy.

When everyone is back, you will share with your partner and tell him or her what happened and what the missing power animal is. Afterwards, you will switch places with your partner. So, if you were the Shaman you will now be the healee. We will repeat the exercise.

EXPERIENCES OF MARY K FOR DOROTHY: Once the drum started, there was a wolf beside me who took me down a tree trunk into the Underworld. There were caves and glens. I saw a snake and another wolf. The third wolf was standing by the entrance to a cave. I checked by asking my guides if the wolf was Dorothy's missing power animal. The wolf had a lot of white on the neck and chest and shoulders. I asked the wolf, whose nose was in my face, what message he had for Dorothy. His message was that he was bringing strength and wisdom, so that Dorothy could enjoy greater self-belief. He said that she was well on her spiritual journey — much further than she believes.

DOROTHY: I saw the wolf before he was blown into me. I let the imagery go because I wasn't supposed to be in it. I allowed whatever animal was to come to me to come.

EXPERIENCE OF DOROTHY FOR MARY K: My mind kept trying to get in the way. I went down the slide, which is how I like to go. I saw a porcupine, and then a rabbit came.

The rabbit was black and brown. Then the porcupine came again, as did the rabbit. I swung around on a rope and came back down again. There was the rabbit. He wouldn't talk to me. What I felt was that you are not to be afraid and move forwards. Rabbits hop along and go forwards.

EXPERIENCE OF TRUDY FOR DENISE: I saw myself as a prairie dog. I went into a hole and came out into a lush, green forest. I saw a brown bird, a donkey, an elephant, the brown bird, and again the brown bird. The bird said that he would like to help Denise fly.

EXPERIENCE OF DENISE FOR TRUDY: I brought back a small, baby deer, like Bambi.

INSTRUCTOR: When the power animal is young, oftentimes, it means that this is a new animal medicine for the individual.

EXPERIENCES OF JOAO FOR PATRICIA: I went down and met a dog. I walked away and saw a crocodile. When I asked him if he was Joao's missing power animal, he answered no, as did the weasel. While I was looking, the dog came and put his paw on me.

EXPERIENCE OF PATRICIA FOR JOAO: I went down an elevator. When I reached the Underworld I was surrounded by a group of small dogs. They were all wagging their tails. When I asked if one was Joao's missing power animal they said no. I walked on and saw a giraffe and a horse. In the background I kept seeing a persistent black panther. When I asked if he was Joao's missing power animal he told me, "I will

188

give my wild power to Joao so that he might use it in healing and the Shamanic work he does."

EXPERIENCE OF KATHLEEN FOR FRANK: I went down and saw a horse. I asked if this was for Frank. I was told that while Frank would benefit from the power of horse, he needed more. I continued on and a wolf came to me. I asked the same question. I was told that while Frank would benefit from the teaching qualities of wolf, he needed more. Then a great husky appeared. This time when I asked the same question, I was told that husky had similar qualities of both horse and wolf. Husky was Frank's missing power animal.

EXPERIENCE OF FRANK FOR KATHLEEN: I saw a few animals and then I saw porcupine. In his innocence he brings faith and trust.

EXPERIENCES OF ANTHONY FOR DONNIE: I was with Donnie, as a young boy with his friends. We all ran around and played in the pine straw. One of the boys brushed the pine straw aside and drew a raccoon in the dirt. I asked if the raccoon was the power animal but it wasn't. The power animal was an owl, who explained his powers. He said, "I am the power animal you are looking for because I possess stillness of mind, knowledge, wisdom, understanding and contemplation."
I asked, "Is this the only power animal that I am to bring back for Donnie?"
A bluebird presented himself and said, "I am the bluebird of happiness." It was innocent and cheerful in its song.

EXPERIENCES OF DONNIE FOR ANTHONY: I slide down the slide and it took a minute for me to focus when I got there. I cleared myself and said, "Power animal please come forward."

In the distance a lion turned his head and looked at me. When I asked him if he was Anthony's power animal, he disappeared and a big, beautiful white tiger appeared. The tiger got in my face and licked my face. I asked him, "Why are you the power animal?"

He said, "For love and courage."

EXPERIENCES OF VICKIE FOR KATHLEEN: I had my guide take me to a place where there were lots of animals. Some of the notable ones included a beautiful white owl — just gorgeous! I saw a goat three times. Then I saw a fish three times. So I asked, "Why is the fish the power animal?"

The fish came out of the water and said, "I am not!"

I turned and looked at the goat again and asked, "Why are you the power animal?"

He said, "Because I am friendly, you can touch and pet me. I am sure-footed on slippery slopes; I am gentle but I pack a powerful punch." I thanked him and brought him back.

EXPERIENCE OF KATHLEEN FOR VICKIE: I saw myself walking towards a tree, but the tree was small and in the middle of the drum that you were beating. I asked, "What is this?"

I was told that it was the World Tree and couldn't help remarking, "This is a pretty small World Tree."

I was told that the World Tree is just beginning to come back to Mother Earth.

190

Also, that I was to travel down the World Tree that was in the drum to the Underworld to look for Vickie's missing power animal.

I asked, "How am I to do this? The tree is very small!" Either I became smaller or the tree became bigger. I found an opening and went down the roots. I was aware that something else went down with me. When we came out, I looked at my companions. The only thing that comes close to describing them was that they looked like upright standing, small elephant-like creatures. But they were not miniature elephants.

I started looking around for Vickie's missing power animal when a large elephant appeared. She was wearing a magnificent jeweled headdress. Then I found myself on the back of the elephant. Because I was concerned that I just had elephants on my mind, I told the elephant, "If you are Vickie's power animal, you are going to have to prove it to me." To my surprise just then, two more elephants appeared walking behind us. Elephants can clear or move anything. In African lore, elephant, not lion, is the king of the Otherworld.

I brought back the elephant with the jeweled headdress for Vickie.

From Tera, My Journey Home here is an example of how an animal that is not an individual's power animal may help:

It is an interesting fact of reincarnation that we are not only drawn to those and that, which we love, but also to those whom we hate. In Ireland, there are many reincarnations of former popes. Most of them, like Kathleen Dillan, are so guilty that they cannot let go of their need for self-punishment. She also had a need to be in control of the healings she facilitated. In one Shamanic Workshop, Kathleen Dillan found a comrade in Crocodile. At one point in the class when we were using journeywork to do a healing, Crocodile held Kathleen so that she could not look to see what was happening and control the outcome. She was being forced to "Let go and let God work!"

Sometimes, people need to feel the pain before it can be released. When it was Kathleen Dillan's turn to receive hands-on healing from the class, she realized that she had been a pope and that she was responsible for the torture and burning of thousands upon thousands of people (including children). Then she flipped into a past life where she was being burned as a witch. Her agony went on and on. She repeatedly refused to forgive herself. Then, I finally said to her in a very calm, gentle voice, "OK, if that's what you want, then keep on burning."

Kathleen Dillan answered, "Wait a minute. What was it that you said I needed to do?"

"You need to forgive yourself! Would you like the angels to come in and help you?"

She said, "No angels."

"Whom would you accept to come in and help you?"

Her response was "Crocodile!"

Crocodile came in, laid over her and began talking to her. "I have

eaten many people. Let go of your
anguish and guilt. Just don't do it
again!" Kathleen Dillan laughed and
broke her reincarnation cycle of
destruction and self-inflicted
torture.

As an introduction to the next
chapter, here is an excerpt from Reiki &
Other Rays of Touch Healing:

Sometimes a past life surfaces
for a client after I get an
impression. I was working on a woman
at Ishpiming when I received the name,
"Constantine." As there are relatively
few 'famous people' in history, my
left brain jumped in and said
emphatically, "No!" but the name,
Constantine, came again. Feeling the
power of the woman's spirit under my
hands, my left brain conjured the
possibility that perhaps this was one
of Constantine's generals. The name
Constantine persistently repeated, and
I reluctantly spoke the name to my
client. Her eyes opened like a shot.
She was amazed that I had picked up
what she had known for most of her
life. Ever since she was three years
old, she had cried irrepressible tears
at every new and every full moon.
Thus far, she had found that
Transcendental Meditation was the only
method of controlling her
uncontrollable remorse. From the time
she could first remember, she carried
within her heart what felt like a
heavy object. This battle-weary
warrior longed to return to the Light
and trusted that I had released my own

judgments and was channeling the healing energy she needed to heal. As past lives were being healed during the session, I pulled off many past-life cloaks and garb, which represented the shedding of and healing of old issues. Included in her etheric closet were many red hats, as well as a pontiff hat. However, there was one particular bishop's hat and the lifetime she led while wearing that hat that was too familiar to me. In the moment, I realized that this man had had me burned alive as a witch; I could actually feel singeing smoke in my lungs. Her friend and one of my students, who were observing the process, later told me that my face went white when I saw the bishop's hat. They had expected me to either start choking her or throw her off of the table. Instead, I helped her to release her guilt and explained to her that many ascended masters had lived lifetimes as warriors and even black magicians before they returned to the Light. As Constantine and the many past lives between then and now were healed, the smoke cleared out of my lungs. Because I put aside judgments and aided my 'enemy', great healing came to me. Straight Arrow told me that I would never fully be conscious of the rewards bestowed upon me because of this single act of compassion. Your enemies may or may not come to you for healing or forgiveness; if they do, heaven will reward you too for your generosity of compassion.

Soul Retrieval

The soul may fragment during trauma - rape, child abuse, a car wreck, war or other stressful, fearful, agonizing times. For example, a soldier suffering from post-war trauma may appear dazed and 'not himself'. His friends and family may say that he is a different person, or his personality is gone or changed drastically. There are people, who were sexually abused as children who do not remember. The part of the personality that suffered the abuse may separate in such a way that the rest of the personality is unaware that the violations took place.

Soul retrieval begins exactly like power animals retrieval: The Shaman lies down next to the healee so that one of her/his shoulders touches one of the shoulders of the healee. While someone beats the drum, the Shaman journeys into the Otherworlds. S/he sees her/himself clearly in her/his mind's eye standing in a beautiful place in nature. S/he looks for an opening into the Underworld.

Traditionally, when the Shaman reaches the Underworld s/he calls upon her/his power animal(s) to help him find the healee's soul fragment. The soul fragment may look like the individual at the time the shock took place, or it might be an object that represents the healee or something belonging to the healee. The Shaman takes the soul fragment to her/his heart, returns to the physical world and blows the soul fragment into the heart chakra (over sternum) and third eye of the healee.

The problem is that the trauma is also blown into the healee. The idea being that the personality has grown enough that the healee is now strong enough to work through the emotional and mental complications that were caused by the stress. Needless to say, soul retrieval has not been a popular choice of therapy.

This is the reason why healing initiations are given in the first part of the class. If a Shaman is channeling healing energy then after the Shaman finds the soul fragment, s/he takes the soul fragment to a place of healing. How does the Shaman know where to take the soul fragment? S/he asks her/his power animal(s) what to do and where to go! A soul fragment may require more than one kind of healing. The idea is to keep asking the power animal(s).

When the Shaman is channeling healing energy, soul retrieval may be expanded to include past lives whereby the personality lived a quite dastardly life. Thus, the soul did not fragment through trauma, but rather through grievous deeds of the personality. In these cases, the past life personality in that lifetime has remained earthbound in a dark, gloomy nightmare of its own making. Deeds that cause such dreadful afterlife conditions include the practice of black magic, murder, incest, political and judicial corruption, greed, ruination of an innocent individual, etc.

INSTRUCTOR: You will find a different partner. Choose who is going to be the Shaman and who is going to be the healee. You will lie down or sit next to one another in such a way that your shoulders or knees are touching one another. When I

196

begin beating the drum, the healee will stay here in meditation.

Shaman, when I begin beating the drum you will see yourself clearly in your mind's eye standing in a beautiful place in nature. You will look for an opening into the Underworld. Travel into the Underworld and begin looking for your partner's soul fragment. Ask the spirit helpers or power animals in the Underworld to help you. You may find a soul fragment from this lifetime or another lifetime. You may find that soul fragment looking as the individual did in that period of his or her life. Or you may find that the soul fragment is represented by a visual metaphor.

After you find the soul fragment ask your guides where to take the soul fragment for healing. Follow their instructions. After the soul fragment has been healed, hold out your physical and etheric hands and allow the soul fragment to come into your hands. Bring your etheric and physical hands back to your chest, gently holding the soul fragment in your cupped hands. Come back the same way in which you went down. Blow the soul fragment into the healee's heart chakra and third eye. Clap your hands or click your fingers to ground the healing.

Sometimes, you may find a soul fragment being held captive by creatures that do not appear negative. Sometimes, these creatures will give up the soul fragment to you readily. Other times, they may not! In such cases you may ask the creatures what they would like in exchange for the soul fragment, or ask your power animals what to do. Sometimes, these creatures are taking advantage of the situation in a good way to get something they want. Whatever these creatures want will be provided to you. On the other hand, if negative spirits are holding a dark soul captive, again ask your power animals what to do. Simply know that if you have found a fragmented soul or personality, it is ready to be released. It is your job to work with the power animals and spirit helpers to release and heal the soul fragment or personality.

When everyone is back you will share with your partner what happened and which soul fragment you brought back with you. Afterwards, you will switch places with your partner. So, if you were the Shaman you will now be the healee. We will repeat the exercise.

MARY K FOR DOROTHY: Immediately, I went down through the earth and came out onto a beach. I sat on a little shell and then went down to the seabed. There were lots of seahorses dancing around in a circle. Inside the circle was a little girl in a blue gingham dress. She was very sad. I asked the seahorses if I could join them. They welcomed me and I became a part of the circle. I asked if the girl could join us and they said, "No, she is our toy." The girl was crying.

I asked the seahorses, "May I swap toys with you?" A pink Barbie doll with diamonds appeared. The seahorses were overjoyed.

I asked my guides where to take the little girl, and they said to take her to her mother. We went to the mother, who was cooking and ignoring her daughter. I asked my guides where to take the girl for healing. We went to a playground, but it was not enough. Then we went to the seaside. I was told that the energy of the water was important for the little girl.

When the healing was completed, I asked again what to do with the little girl. We ended up back with her mom. The little girl again tugged at her mom's apron. Still the mom did not pay attention. So, the little girl went around to the front of her mom, stepping into her way. This time, the little girl sent love and then the mom sent love back. The room was filled with pink love light. I asked if there was something else to do. I was told to surround them both with angels. I did! Then I returned and blew the little girl surrounded by pink into Dorothy.

DOROTHY FOR MARY K: I went down and saw this black swirl. There was a lot of energy. I found myself going up to a large house with columns. Then a horse and rider came to the house. They were carrying Mary K. Then I did not see you. Then I saw you in the house, lying down exhausted in your bed. I felt that you had been thrown from place to place, and that you had been in dark water. I asked what to do next. All I could see was the tornado. I asked Mary K if she wanted to leave this house. She said, "Yes."

We walked out of the house and into a coloring book, where we recreated that page of Mary K's life. The angels helped and when we were done, the angels said that they were always there to help. This memory is no longer a part of your reality.

Mary K, have you ever been Dorothy in a school play of <u>The Wizard of Oz</u>?

MARY K: No but I have dreamed of being Dorothy.

199

INSTRUCTOR: When an individual has dreams of being in a tornado, it may mean that s/he is in a negative cycle from which there appears absolutely no way out. Now that you are freed from the tornado, you are left with the magic red slippers. That is, your trials have made you strong so that you are able to exit situations before they turn into tornados. You are also able to help others to do the same.

EXPERIENCE OF TRUDY FOR KATHLEEN: My power animal, Bambi, came to me. He took me to a Canadian landscape. There were large hardwood trees, magnificent mountains and a wide river. We saw a red ruby. Bambi told me that I had to swim back and forth across the river with the ruby to clean it. When I asked if there was something else we might do to clean the ruby, Bambi told me to crush it. When I did that, I felt deep emotional pain being released.

EXPERIENCE OF DENISE FOR PATRICIA: I sat on the brown bird. We flew over the trees to a house. There was a swing, but there was something wrong. I had to cut the swing down and burn the poles. Then I gave the swing back to Patricia.

INSTRUCTOR: Science has proven that both water and wood hold memory.

EXPERIENCE OF JOAO FOR FRANK: I was disorientated, but managed to make it down the slide to the Underworld. When I arrived I was dizzy. My black panther and I began looking for Frank's soul fragment. A talking, chattering monkey passed us. We came upon a river, where a falcon waited. My black panther told me to give water to the falcon. I was told that this healing will give Frank speed.

EXPERIENCE OF PATRICIA FOR DENISE: I met my golden retriever. He stopped a few times. We passed a little girl who said that she was not Denise's soul fragment. Then I saw a beautiful red rose. When I asked if this was Denise's soul fragment it said, "Yes!"

I put it under a shower with crabapple remedy.

EXPERIENCES OF VICKIE FOR DONNIE: My power animal appeared and I asked for additional help to find the missing soul fragment. We went down a cloudy tunnel; there was a bright fire at the bottom of it. When I reached the bottom there was a brown sparrow with bright sparkles of blue and teal, and a little bit of purple and white. The sparrow was not the missing soul fragment. She flew away, but in the nest was an egg. The egg opened and inside was a ring. When I asked, I was told that the ring represented the missing soul fragment.

I picked up the ring. The band was thin, like a lady's ring. On half of the ring there was a metal flower petal design with a large, yellow, luminous, speckled stone in the middle of it. The other half had a closed metal flower petal design. I was told to take it to the woods. In the middle of the woods there was a stream that glimmered with yellow and blue light. I put the ring into the stream and watched a white flower come up. I asked if the ring was clean and was told, "No, where you are holding the ring it is still tarnished."

I put the ring back into the water and held it down until another white flower came up. When I asked if the ring was healed, I was told, "No!"

So, I went up into the sky to a worm tunnel. I went through the worm tunnel to another universe that had Egyptian-like symbology. The fire there was clear. I was told to throw the ring into the fire. When the cartoon-type stars came and surrounded it, I was told that the ring was ready.

EXPERIENCES OF DONNIE FOR VICKIE: As soon as I closed my eyes I saw wagons drawn by horses. It scared me. Everything freezes, including a guy standing on a covered wagon. Suddenly, I am on the back of an elephant. I asked, "If I am where I am supposed to be, trumpet." The elephant responded with a big blow out its trunk.

The horses kept coming straight towards me. Just before they reached me the horses suddenly turn to the right and the wagon falls over. A little girl of about four fell out the back and tumbled across the ground. She was screaming and crying, and she had the cutest little rag doll. Two people that had been on the wagon were dead. Two other people walked up to the overturned wagon, looked around and then took off without the girl. They left her!

I asked, "Is this the soul fragment I am to retrieve for Vickie?" The next thing I know, I am picking up the girl. She sat behind me on the elephant. I asked, "How do we clean the girl?" Then it started raining, and I mean raining. Sheet after sheet after sheet of rain, came down at angles! Everything was soaked. The girl climbed over me and stood on the head of the elephant. I held her up and said, "Be cleansed!" She spun around and gave me a

202

big hug. I told her, "You will never be alone again."

EXPERIENCES OF ANTHONY FOR KATHLEEN: I started off in the woods and saw an eagle flying. My white tiger came and told me to get on its back. We galloped for a while. When we came to a lake, he jumped into the water and swam for quite a distance. We climbed out onto the shore. In a flash, I saw a horse. Then I saw a small, dark, expressionless, Moroccan man. Next to him appeared a baby, who was old enough to sit down and play with things in front of the old man. Then I saw a blond-haired little girl on a white horse. She had her arms around the horse's neck and her head resting on the horse's mane. The Moroccan man and baby were still there. I asked the tiger what to do. He said, "Take them into your hands and cleanse them."

I took them to a waterfall. For the first time, the baby was happy. Instead of a dry and gray expression, the gentleman was warm. I couldn't come to any logical conclusion about who they were and what was happening. When the tiger told me that the healing was completed, I brought them back and blew them into Kathleen's heart chakra and third eye.

INSTRUCTOR: The thing about the Otherworlds is that logic does not work. If something befuddles you, ask your power animal what is going on. However, you may still not receive the logic you seek. Journeys in the Otherworlds are like dreams in this respect.

EXPERIENCE OF KATHLEEN FOR ANTHONY: Immediately, I saw the back of a high priest, who had a lot of power. The man shape-shifted between looking like Anthony does at this moment, to a middle-aged man with a thick, graying braid down the middle of his back. He was working on some kind of magical ceremony. I asked if this was it, and received the answer, "Yes, here he is!"

The man required a lot of healing. At one point, I was asked to heal a bracelet that had three, large turquoise-colored stones in it. Two of the gems fell out, leaving dirty black holes. The spirit guides cleaned out the holes and put new stones in the holes. Even as the stones were being placed in the bracelet, more black came oozing out. More healing was required, so, they put you into water. You had your back to a wooden barrier, which was holding you back. After a while, three beautiful, white lotus flowers floated by. They pushed against the barrier and the water began to flow again. There were more healings that you went through; however, those were the two biggest.

I was just about ready to bring you back when another man appeared. I asked him who he was. He answered that he was another one of your past lives and was taking advantage of the healing opportunity. He was a red-haired knight. When I asked what to do, I was told to simply hold him between my hands. When he was healed, I came back, and blew them both into your heart and third eye.

INSTRUCTOR: Scientists recently discovered an energetic membrane that connects us to everything else in our universe. Spiritually speaking, this is God's presence. This is one of the reasons why healings and readings are possible.

Retrieving Information from the Otherworlds

Thoughts, like energy, do not disappear. There is a stream of consciousness, so that it is possible to go backwards and retrieve information. In addition to this, thoughts carry themselves to their logical conclusion. Some things are destined to be; for example, John Kennedy was destined to become President and die in office. Nostradamas said that this prediction was inevitable. Readings from the Akashic Records are preordained. Other readings are how things will happen if events are not altered; something like the warning that the Spirit of Christmas Yet to Come gave Scrooge. These readings are legitimate. Then there are psychics who read the thought forms and wishes in the aura — these thoughts and wishes do not typically come into form as they appear, or they may alter or not manifest at all.

INSTRUCTOR: You will write a question that you do not mind being read to the group. One question only! Not, *"Will I move to another country and begin a new business?"* That is two questions, not one! Bring the paper to me unfolded. You may watch! I will fold them so that they are identical and put them into a container. You will each pick one piece of paper, which you will leave folded! You will not look at or read the question. Simply hold the piece of paper in your hand.

When I begin beating the drum you will see yourself clearly in your mind's eye standing in a beautiful place in nature. You will look for an opening into the Underworld. You will look for your power animal and ask, "What is the answer to this question?" If what you receive is unclear you may ask, "Please clarify this." Or "Please show me the answer in another way."

If you see visuals but do not hear the answer or have an inner knowing as to what the answer is, you will only share what you saw with the individual who wrote the question. If you try to figure out visuals with your left or logical brain you will 'mess up' the reading. A lot of psychics make this mistake. Instead, ask the individual who asked the question, "Does this mean anything to you?" An impression or the answer might come later.

We will all do this. I will go first so as to take the apprehension out of the experience. If I can beat the drum, journey and find an answer, your job will seem that much easier. I will tell the group what I saw, as well as what I heard or had an inner knowing of. I will then read the question and the name of the individual who wrote the question. He or she will tell me if the answer I received makes any sense. We will continue around the room and you will each have an opportunity to share.

KATHLEEN's READING: I went down into the Otherworlds and the first thing I saw was a horse like Mel; chestnut with a white face. Then there was a foal next to him, who also had a white face. The thought crossed my mind that I had my own question, but I wasn't sure where that came from —

probably my left brain. Just because I am seeing horses doesn't necessarily mean it is my question; after all, Mary K is involved with horses.

So, I went deeper into meditation and asked, "Show this to me in another way." This time I saw two horses, again like Mel, who were pulling a wagon. I asked again and saw a man getting on a horse and riding away — this horse did not look like Mel.

Then I saw myself quite clearly with a light tan pony with a lighter mane and tail. The horse had a stalk of herbs in its mane. I was fooling around with the herbs and her right ear when the pony turned into Duchess. At that I stopped asking.

MARY K's QUESTION — Will I publish more than one book?

MARY K: Your answer does make sense because Heidi and I are talking about breeding mares. As you talked about the horses pulling a wagon, I could see a wagon full of pages. Also, you keep seeing the horses in twos, and I think that I am to write two books.

DOROTHY's READING: I never could get a clear read, but I saw underbrush with animals scurrying around. I swung out several times and saw the float with somebody on the float near the beach. I went up but I could not tell if the water was shrinking or just flowing through. At one time, it looked like an island off of Greece. I couldn't get much else.

DOROTHY DREW HER OWN QUESTION: What kind of healing work will I do once I retire?

MARY K's READING: I went down through a blade of grass and up into a woodland. One particular cave was shining brightly in front of me. It was a tall cave. On either side of it were giant, golden guardian angels. I asked them, "What do you mean?"

They answered, "We are here to help."

"Who are you?"

"Medatron and Sandalphon!" They are twins. They are the only angels whose names do not end in 'iel'. They were once earthbound but managed to elevate themselves.

In between their wings stood Pegasus. I asked if they could show me the answer to the question.

"The desired outcome is much closer than you think. Call on the three of us. Ask us to help."

My rabbit took me back up to the Earth level.

KATHLEEN's QUESTION: Is it in my horses' and my best interest to move them to _____'s farm before I go to Europe in September?

KATHLEEN's FOLLOW UP: I asked Medatron, Sandalphon and Pegasus to watch over my horses while I was gone for the month. The farm in question did not work out; I believe it would have been worse had I not been praying to those angels. The next farm didn't work out either and I kept asking the three winged angels for help. Then I was guided through a series of incredible, near-miss events to the right stable. Nancy Moore, who went looking with me on December 1st, said that surely spirit was guiding us. Maybe the angels?

208

KATHLEEN's READING: I went into the Otherworld and saw a mole digging a horizontal tunnel. He stopped when he came to a group of white Roman-type soldiers holding white spears and white shields. I had no feeling or answer as to what it was that I was seeing.

So, I asked to see the answer in another way. Then I saw myself holding the question up to the light, but there was no answer! I simply stood there looking at the question.

So, I asked to see the answer in yet another way. The question was put on a clothesline. The question on the clothesline was then fed to Patricia.

DENISE's QUESTION: Unfortunately it did not make sense in English.

PATRICIA: When I translate Denise's question into Dutch, it doesn't make sense either.

DENISE: I was actually thinking of another question when I wrote this one.

INSTRUCTOR: It is important to concentrate and be clear when asking a question, whose answer is in the Otherworlds. Probably good advise for this world as well!

READING BY VICKIE: I asked my power animal, the elephant, what the answer to the question was. I felt the elephant sniffing and snuffeling the question in my left hand. I walked with the elephant. We saw several things. When I asked the elephant if these were relevant to the question, the elephant answered, "No!"

When I asked what was relevant, a drawing appeared in much the same way a picture is downloaded on a computer. However, the picture of the man appeared from the bottom going up. He had cowboy boots on, old-fashioned pants and he was dancing. His belt and shirt were also western garb. Over this he wore a duster and he had a hat on his head. His face, however, was a mountain lion-type face, but he had catfish-type whiskers. I asked him, "What is the answer to this question?"

He reached into the inside pocket of his duster with his right hand and pulled out a roll of money. The picture started to fade, and I could see that there was a bright jewel that he held in his fingertips. Everything faded out except for the pure, shimmering light of the diamond.

VICKIE'S QUESTION: What is the purpose for my incarnation in this lifetime?

READING BY DONNIE: I asked my two power animals, owl and bluebird, "What is the answer to this question?" The bluebird sat on my shoulder and we flew behind the owl to a forest. I was not allowed in the forest, I could only stand back and watch. There was a simple cabin in the forest. There was a fire outside and a male Native American danced around the fire. He danced so long that he wore a circular groove around the fire. I asked, "Is this what I am to see?" The owl nodded his head.

I said, "OK! I don't understand. You will have to show me the answer in a different way." He took me in front of the house, about two or three feet from the front porch steps. The door swung open and there was a person sweeping out dust and junk and paper off the floor. Sparkles came out of the dust. I asked, "Is the answer for the person to continue sweeping out her/his house?" A feeling of peace came with that. I wanted to be sure, so, I asked, "If this is true, show me in one more way."

I was taken to a barn. The barn door flew open and I saw somebody cleaning out the stalls. I got the feeling that the person was not exactly happy.

ANTHONY'S QUESTION: What am I to learn from my mother's incarnation?

ANTHONY'S READING: I went down and saw a gentlemanly, Tarzan-type jungle man. He was swinging from vine to vine with a monkey. The momentum stopped when another vine failed to appear. Tarzan and the monkey still held onto the vine, removing the leaves from the vine as they went down. They landed on a neat pile of leaves, which were the leaves that had come off the vine as they dropped down. Tarzan picked up all of the leaves in his left hand. The leaves turned into stacks of money. In his other hand he held three small, young, white coconuts. The monkey grabbed the money and threw it up into the air, and it landed on the ground. Then the monkey took the coconuts one at a time and threw them on the ground. The first coconut broke, and out came golden coins. Silver coins came out of the second coconut. Darkish, deep blue, translucent, powerful disks came out of the third coconut. In the midst of all of this the monkey starts doing backflips.

KATHLEEN'S QUESTION: Will I be moving my horses to another stable December 1st, or is there a better place for them?

211

KATHLEEN: You were right on target! Since moving to North Carolina in May, I have had my horses at three different stables in six months. As stated earlier, I did find the right stable on December 1st.

Sometimes, the meaning of the reading is immediately apparent. Other times, the meaning will come later with a sudden knowing. Or the answer may come in a dream.

KATHLEEN's READING: I went into the Underworld and found a brown bear, but he wasn't totally like a real bear. He was something between a Shrek-type bear and a real brown bear. Then I saw a lady's hand. Three bright, shiny rings were placed on her fingers. I began walking and everything turned white. I found myself inside of a beautiful white flower. Then I saw a dark, billowy square that was divided into four parts by two sketchy, white lines. In the middle of the square a diamond appeared. It turned out to be a portal. I went through the tunnel and up to the clouds and found an angel behind a counter. I asked the angel, "What is the answer to this question?"

The angel pulled out a disk that turned and became a hoop. Then I saw Anthony. I didn't know if it was because I had Anthony's question or he had mine. Then food was being handed to nurture people.

DONNIE'S QUESTION: Will my thoughts and goals for healing be successful?

KATHLEEN: What you begin may surprisingly lead to something else.

Facilitating Healings from the Otherworld

Mathew: Chapter 10: And having called his twelve disciples together, he gave them power over unclean spirits, to cast them out, and to heal all manner of diseases, and all manner of infirmities.

Those who say that healing is the work of the devil quote Mathew: Chapter 7: Verses 22 & 23: Many will say to me in that day: Lord, Lord, have not we prophesied in thy name, and cast out devils in they name, and done many miracles in they name. And then will I profess unto them, I never knew you: depart from me, you that work iniquity.

Sounds like a serious contradiction until all of the facts are revealed. Mathew: Chapter 7 is a continuation of the Sermon on the Mount and begins with the phrase, "Judge not that you may not be judged." Another popular quote from this chapter are verses 7 & 8. "Ask and it shall be given you: seek, and you shall find: knock and it shall be opened to you. For every one that seeketh, findeth: and to him that knocketh, it shall be opened."

One way to misinform people is to selectively quote and take things out of context. Mathew: Chapter 7: Verses 15 – 21 have a significant bearing on Mathew: Chapter 7: Verses 22 & 23.

Mathew: Chapter 7: Verses 15 – 21: Beware of false prophets, who come to you in the clothing of sheep, but inwardly they are ravening wolves. By their fruits you shall know them. Do men gather grapes of thorns, or figs of thistles? Even so every good tree bringeth forth good fruit, and the evil tree bringeth forth evil fruit. A good tree cannot bring forth evil fruit, neither can an evil tree bring forth good fruit. Every tree that bringeth not forth good fruit, shall be cut down, and shall be cast into the fire. Wherefore by their fruits you shall know them. Not every one that saith to me, Lord, Lord, shall enter into the kingdom of heaven: but he that doth the will of my Father who is in heaven, he shall enter into the kingdom of heaven.

Healings facilitated by a Shaman in the Otherworlds are not hands-on healing. Rather, such healings use the power of the third eye and the healing energy that the Shaman is channeling. All healing comes from God; the Shaman's spirit helpers guide Shamanic healings. Shamanic healings are conducted in the presence of the healee or absentee. When the healee is present, the Shaman might lie down next to the healee so that they might touch shoulders.

INSTRUCTOR: You will find a different partner. Choose who is going to be the Shaman and who is going to be the healee. Healee, you will tell your Shaman what physical, mental or emotional issues you would like him or her to work on. You will both lie down or sit next to one another in such a way that your shoulders or knees are touching one another. When I begin beating the drum, the healee will stay here in meditation.

Shaman, when I begin beating the drum you will see yourself clearly in your mind's eye standing in a beautiful place in nature. You will look for an opening into the Underworld. Travel into the Underworld and begin looking for the power animals and spirit helpers, who will help you do the healing. You may find yourself gathering herbs or crystals, you may go directly to the healee, or something else will happen. Ask your power animals and spirit helpers questions, such as: What am I to do? How am I to do it? Is there something else we might do to help?

You may watch the angels, power animals or spirit helpers work. You may become very small and go inside of an organ, gland, bone, etc. You may only see a particular organ, gland, bone, etc. You may see the whole person. You may see the etheric organ or gland rise up out of the individual. When this occurs the body part is usually blue in color.

It is most important that you see yourself and watch what happens! If you move your etheric hands, it often helps to move your physical hands as well. You may be asked to come back and bring with you herbs to blow into the body. There are loads of possibilities.

When everyone has finished, each Shaman will have the opportunity to share her/his experiences. Partners may also share their experiences. Physical changes may occur during or after the journey. After sharing, you will switch roles with your partner, and the exercise will be repeated.

Healings may be done to release black magic, evil enchantments or thought forms that have outlived their usefulness from someone or the Earth. Before going on the journey you may be impressed to draw the infinity symbol, or a symbol of healing in the air or on the palms of your hands. In the case of black magic, when you reach the Underworld you will want to wear a silver cloak of invisibility (J. K. Rawlings is correct — silver is the color of invisibility.) Afterwards, you might ask the angels to set up a divergence. It is important to stay out of judgment with the black magician. If you get into judgment, you run the risk of being pulled into the game - becoming like what you judge.

EXPERIENCE OF KATHLEEN FOR PATRICIA: Patricia asked me to work on her joints. When I went into the Underworld I saw Patricia's left arm; it was black. I was asked to pull blackness out of the bones and joints. At one point during the healing, Patricia stood up and stepped out of a dark, turtle-like shell. At another point, she was only a skeleton with cartilage. I was asked to work on her entire skeleton and all of her connective tissue.

PATRICIA: I felt nauseous and there was a ringing in my ear when the healing began. Both symptoms persisted for five to ten minutes and then left. I could feel my joints being worked on.

EXPERIENCE OF PATRICIA FOR KATHLEEN: I went down and you stood there waiting for me. Then you laid down upon a bed of herbs and flowers. My power animal laid on your

216

spine. I balanced your hips — you needed a lot of energy there.

KATHLEEN: I could feel you both working on me.

FOLLOW UP: During the ensuing five months after the Shamanic journey Patricia did for me, I kept running into incidents that brought healing to my hips from the car injury.

EXPERIENCE OF FRANK FOR DENISE: Denise wanted me to help her stop smoking. When I went down into the Underworld, I was told that she needed the will to stop smoking. I took her into nature and filled her lungs with fresh air. Then I put my hands on her chest — front and back.

EXPERIENCE OF DENISE FOR FRANK: When I went into the Underworld and found Frank, I felt an unpleasant feeling in my left side. We went into a church where I cleaned Frank with spiritual objects.

INSTRUCTOR: Sometimes, the Shaman receives awareness in her/his body where the problem is in the healee's body. It is a wonderful guide to help the Shaman know where to look. Some Shaman experience the pain that the healee is having; if this is the case, ask your angels, spirit guides and power animals to substitute pain for awareness in your body.

EXPERIENCE OF JOAO FOR TRUDY: Trudy told me that she had had an operation on her left foot. When I went down into the Underworld, my black panther and I found Trudy right away, but I could not see anything wrong with her foot. My black panther told me that Trudy's foot needed time to heal. He suggested that I put my hands on Trudy — she took a lot of energy. My black panther told Trudy, "You may place your foot on my belly."

EXPERIENCE OF TRUDY FOR JOAO: I saw a big castle and Bambi. Together we took Joao into the castle garden. Joao's black panther came and put his tail inside of Joao's chest. Bambi said, "I'm going to ask all of the healers and their power animals to help you."

Bambi wanted me to put my hands on Joao's head in order to lighten it. At the end of the healing Joao was blessed.

JOAO: I felt a lot working inside me.

KATHLEEN — EMOTIONAL HEALING FOR DONNIE: I saw a woman but only from the neck down. She was wearing black negligee. I asked, "What does this mean?" The answer I received was that it had to do with part of your conception of women and your feminine side. So, I asked, "How can this be healed?" A row of four crystal Quan Yens appeared, one behind the other walking down a flight of stairs. A fire appeared in the headdress of the Quan Yen, who was the furthest back. The fire went to the headdress of the second and third Quan Yen. Then the fourth Quan Yen, the one nearest to the front, became real. However, she wore an Indian headdress that was too big for her; it was falling down over her left eye.

The overwhelming feeling I had was that you have an ideal woman in mind; one who is both sexy and into spiritualism in the same way in which you are. However, you might be trying to put the ring or in this case, the headdress, on the wrong woman. Oftentimes, when a man and a woman are in the same field, competition, expectations and jealousy arise. Think about the Hollywood divorces, and also what kinds of couples do not get divorced in Hollywood. You might simply consider asking God for the right woman to come into your life.

There was other symbology that I could not get a clear read on. At one point, there was a mushy chocolate cake in a pan surrounded by milk. The angels cleared the soggy cake away and baked a new chocolate cake. Then they lifted the cake. Under the cake was a shiny figure that could now shine without the cake on top of it.

INSTRUCTOR: The Yin Yang symbol reminds us that there is always an element of feminine in the masculine and conversely, a spot of masculine in the feminine. A man is born with 2/3 masculine energy and 1/3 feminine energy. For women it is the opposite.

DONNIE: There was a time during my healing that I could feel healing energy jump from Kathleen's right leg to my left leg. While I have never had any problems with my legs, something came out of my left leg. I can still feel the healing energy.

INSTRUCTOR: The left side of your body is your feminine side; it is controlled by the intuitive, feminine right brain. The lower legs and feet are the foundation. You are formulating a new feminine groundwork.

219

It also goes to show you that healing does not come out of only the hands.

DONNIE — HEALING KATHLEEN'S HIP: I asked for all of my guides and healers, and all of your guides and healers to come and heal your hip from the car wreck. I asked for the old medicine woman who had come to me yesterday. She worked on your left hip very briefly. She said, "This is all I can do."

I picked you up off the table. A beautiful, amazing white light appeared. Jesus put his arms out. He wanted me to place you in his arms. I initially backed away because of uncomfortable feelings that I have had about Jesus in the past. I put you on the table so that you were sitting up with your legs hanging off one side. Jesus came and started to work on you. Then he asked me to come forward. I hesitated and then stood on the other side of the table. He told me, "Put your hands where I tell you."

I ended up putting my right hand on your right hip and my left hand in the air. Then he had me put both hands on your right hip and pull the energy down. Then I put my right hand back on your right hip and my left hand on your back. Afterwards, he had me massage your feet. Then he had me do quarter circles over your kidneys. Then I touched the back of your head — just a touch. Jesus asked me to come around to his side of the table and stand next to him. I was astonished! I could feel another consciousness coming into my arms. The feeling was incredible! Jesus and the guides and healers stepped back from the table. I found myself with my arms stretched out. You woke up and said, "Thank you!" We bowed to one another.

INSTRUCTOR: Jesus never claimed to be the only Son of God. He said that we were all capable of becoming sons and daughters of God. In 325 AD, Constantine called the First General Council of the Church in Bithynia in a place called Nicaea. It was at this Council of Nicaea that Constantine, Pope Sylvester I, and Church officials voted by only one vote to grant Jesus divinity, thereby proclaiming him to be the only Son of God. The Gnostic Cathari rejected this proclamation, as well other Church doctrines, which they felt went against Jesus' teachings. Rome began a campaign to totally wipe out the Cathari and their beliefs in the first Inquisition. All of this is well documented. Other Christian groups have further distorted some branches of Christianity into a dogmatic, intolerant religion, leaving many with a strong distaste for Jesus. With truth comes understanding and compassion.

ANTHONY — HEALING VICKIE'S EYE: I started in the forest where the medicine cabin is located. I traveled with my white tiger to a clearing. We came to a lake with a huge, jeweled white statue of Buddha in the middle of it. In the eyes of the statue were two, large rubies. Many snakes surrounded the statue. The tiger could not take me to the statue; he said that the snakes did not get along with him. So, I swam out to the statue and climbed it. I touched one of the large rubies. It became smaller and smaller until I could hold it in my hand. I took the ruby back to the tiger and got on his back. He carried me to a place of transmutation, where things could be transmuted and made suitable for the human body. I was taken to the water. I placed the ruby into the water. When I retrieved the ruby, a little glass box came to the surface in the ruby's place. In the glass box was a human eyeball. Electricity from all parts of the box energized the eyeball and kept it suspended so that it did not touch the sides or bottom of the box. I went back to Vickie but I do not remember putting the eyeball into her. The next thing I remember was looking at Vickie and she had two, normal, shining eyes. I was asked to smooth the energy around her, and then she sat up.

VICKIE FOR ANTHONY: I went down and found Anthony lying on a Reiki table. His white tiger and my elephant conferred to determine the cause of Anthony's problem. We left Anthony on the table and walked to a river. A crocodile in the river swam to the bottom. Strangely, there was seaweed in the bottom of the river. He gave me the seaweed, saying that Anthony should eat more seaweed. I took the seaweed back to Anthony and put it in his hand so that I would remember to tell him about it later.

Healers surrounded the table and started to send healing to Anthony. In a short while, a river of water started running through his middle. It took nervous energy out of him to the other side. Crystal and cobalt blue began coming in. Eventually, all of the black atoms in his body exploded. They went up. When the atoms came down, they funneled into the earth to be cleansed.

The healers continued to stand around him touching different parts of his body that needed healing. They put a big white light over his stomach. One of the healers put strong, flexible, clear tubes in Anthony's stomach. Another healer placed a beautiful blue pyramid into Anthony's forehead. I was told to tell Anthony that when his stomach bothers him or he is nervous, that he can visualize the river running through him carrying out pain and nervous energy.

ANTHONY: I could feel her working on my stomach while the drum was beating.

INSTRUCTOR: A Shaman may also energize healing symbols before the journey and take these symbols into the Otherworlds to help with the healing. The Shaman may also hold herbs or flower essences that may be appropriate for the individual's healing. Or place these or other items in the hands of the healee. However, especially in the Shamanic I Class, crystals, essential oils, etc. are usually avoided. It is important for the aspiring Shaman to learn to trust what s/he sees and experiences.

After the Shamanic Class, the Shaman is free to incorporate other healing modalities into her/his journeys. For example, when doing a healing for someone who has passed over, the Shaman may want to hold something the individual owned when s/he was alive. This maybe especially helpful when trying to locate someone who is lost.

In the following two examples, the Shaman took the symbol for release that is in the creativity chapter in this book. This symbol gets to the core issue behind negativity and repeated negative patterns. These issues are brought up to the surface for examination and healing. If the Shaman is also into the tarot, s/he might hold the HERMIT card, as the HERMIT's lantern sheds light onto situations. Or hold the JUSTICE card when seeking to right a wrong. One word of caution, when asking for justice it is wise to ask for compassion as well. In that way, when justice comes to the Shaman, the Shaman will also receive mercy.

JEANIE WARE OF GEORGIA FOR NANCY MOORE: When I went into the Otherworld I saw a huge rock with a crevice. I stepped into the fissure and started to go down. It felt as though layers of old stuff were being shed off of me. I asked for Nancy's guides and angels and my guides and angels to assist in the healing. Then it was as if I was on a coalminer's train, plummeting downwards. I called upon the symbol for RELEASE, and the dark blue healing energy. As soon as I did so, the train came to an abrupt halt.

I stepped off the train. There was a large fireplace and in front of it hung a medallion, with a black & white picture of a man and a little girl. My sense was that it was a picture of Nancy and her father. I asked what this meant, and I was immediately surrounded by fog. So, I asked what the fog meant and how it could be cleared.

The next thing I saw was a train. The man in the picture was on the train. I could see his silhouette, but I knew it was the man in the picture. As a confirmation, I was shown the medallion, which now only held the picture of the child.

I asked what else needed to be done. I was shown a white light with hooks. I watched as the angels removed the hooks and the light became clear.

NANCY MOORE OF NORTH CAROLINA FOR JEANIE WARE: I started off in a field. I made my way to a tree and went into an opening in a bough. I came out into a beautiful field and was met by many animals. We formed a circle. I asked for the angels and spirit beings, who would be able to help with the healing. I called in the dark blue healing energy and the symbol for RELEASE.

I asked what we should do next. Our circle suddenly formed around a small pond. All of us got into the water - it was cool but not cold. When the animals got out of the water I asked what we should do next to help. Immediately, we were all standing around a large fire.

I asked what else we could do to release negativity. The next scenario that appeared was something akin to the Peaceable Kingdom - a lion, a lamb, a leopard and angels. The angels said that if Jeanie ever found herself feeling claustrophobic that she could call upon them and that they would touch her.

SELF-HEALINGS:

INSTRUCTOR: Shaman, when I begin beating the drum you will see yourself clearly in your mind's eye standing in a beautiful place in nature. You will look for an opening into the Underworld. Travel into the Underworld and begin looking for the power animals and spirit helpers, who will help you do a healing for yourself. Rather than you deciding where you will go

and what to do, leave that up to the power
animals, angels and spirit helpers.

EXPERIENCE OF WILLEN BOEREN OF THE
NETHERLANDS: Some negative black energy was
following me. I put on the silver cloak of
invisibility. Wolf and eagle grabbed
blackness, tore it apart, and put it first
into fire and then water. I found myself in
a black hole. I pulled out a golden heart
and prayed to God. I was pulled out of the
hole. Then I was put into the center of the
infinity symbol. My silver cloak was
removed. I was told that I didn't have to
be cloaked.

EXPERIENCE OF MARION VALKENBURGH OF
THE NETHERLANDS: As I was going down, I met
my power animals — rhino and eagle. I was
standing in the middle of a rope. I asked
that it be released. As the rope was pulled
off of me, I spun like a top. When I was
through spinning, the angels put a mountain
of flowers in me. I asked for protection.
All around me appeared little white
flowers.

EXPERIENCE OF JOAO RAMOS OF PORTUGAL:
I don't have much to report. I did see
Willem with a golden light around his neck.
I wasn't feeling well. So, I climbed down
to the water. I had to wash myself free of
black magic. I felt much better. Then I saw
myself as an eagle watching from above.

INSTRUCTOR: Even though Joao was not
aware of it at the time, more than likely
he was helping Willem to clear.

How Are We to Color Outside the Lines When We Can't Locate the Crayons?

BREAKING THROUGH THE ILLUSION THAT CREATIVITY IS DIFFICULT: The left logical brain learns the techniques and information necessary to operate and deal with a variety of important tasks in the physical world. Left-brain learning involves memorization, task completion, formulation, discernment, categorization and the wisdom necessary to function judiciously. The right creative brain receives imaginative and innovative ideas from the World of Spirit or the Otherworld. One of the blockages to creativity is that the left logical brain oftentimes views creative thought as illogical, as oftentimes inspired, ingenious, inventive ideas are.

In an introductory Shamanic Class or Creativity Class the instructor presents graduated tasks in such a way so as to surprise the left brain with information that the right brain picks up from the Otherworlds. The left brain works with conclusive evidence; when information from the right brain works out, the left brain begins to have confidence in right-brained ideas. When the left brain relaxes its stranglehold, the right brain is able to function.

The Creativity Class has nothing to do with grammar, sentence structure or paragraph organization. The objective is to reach the place where creative thought is found, to think outside of the box, and get impressions down on paper. Editorializing comes after artistic inspiration.

It helps if the teacher is both a healer and creative. Her/his creativity may not necessarily be writing; it could well be music or painting. Healing abilities assist in removing blockages; creative skills help inspire people in the class. The teacher's objectives include: 1) Helping workshop participants break down blockages. 2) Helping students feel the narrow etheric channel that originates at the top of the head and culminates in the center of the brain. 3) Stimulating the right brain. 4) Helping students to receive first words and then increasingly complex ideas from outside the brain.

The ability to think outside of the same-old, one-sided view of a narrow range of topics is mandatory for creative thinking. For example, if you are talking and I am only thinking about how I am going to answer or respond to you, I am thinking inside myself. If while you are talking I am actually listening and comprehending what you are saying, I am thinking outside myself.

The initial part of the class is almost solely directed to eradicating obstacles, which act like logjams to imaginative thinking. Issues are chosen that push people's buttons. All of the initial exercises also culminate with the instruction, "Write down the first word that comes to you."

Money is a 'hot' issue for many people. Depak Chopra says that the only people who think more about money than the tremendously rich are the exceptionally poor. Money blockages of the poor are easy to recognize; worrying about not having money stops money from coming in. Many wealthy people fret about losing money, feel they will never have enough money, hold tightly onto their money and exhibit a lack of generosity. These individuals block the flow of money going out. Many former millionaires are reborn in the streets of India. People scoff when they hear that. However, when they meditate on the matter for themselves, they are often surprised at the answer that they receive.

EXERCISE: Students are guided into meditation whereby they experience different forms of wealth. Suggestions are given; such as: Pay attention to how you are feeling in a room filed with gold bullion, coins of the realm, stocks and certificates. Pick up a handful of gold coins. How do they feel in your hand? Feel money coming in and money flowing out. Does it get stuck anywhere?
Towards the end of the meditation the suggestion is given by the instructor: I will ask you five questions. After each question pick up your pen and write down first word or phrase that comes to you. After you write down the word or phrase, set your pen back down and go back into a

slight meditative state. The words and phrases may or may not make sense.

- How do I feel about money?
- How do I treat money?
- What's blocking me from abundance?
- How might I release the blockage?
- How may I have more money?

As the workshop participants share their responses, the teacher works to clear them. Oftentimes, the entire group receives a healing while only one individual's needs are being addressed. Afterwards, students are guided back into the 'money room' to see if their experiences with gold bullion, coins of the realm, stocks and certificates are different. Towards the end of the meditation the suggestion is given: I will ask you a few questions. After each question pick up your pen and write down first word or phrase that comes to you. After you write down the word or phrase, set your pen back down and go back into a slight meditative state. The words and phrases may or may not make sense.

- Is the money blockage gone?
- What else is required?
- I think money is _____

Again the workshop participants share their responses while the teacher works to clear them. The teacher asks, "Did you feel warm energy dripping from the top of your head into the center of your brain through a short, narrow passageway with the diameter of a darning needle?" Even though it is early in the class, there will be people who were able to feel it.

Class exercises progress from writing down what is received in various forms of meditative states to more familiar conscious states. What we think of as

230

conscious isn't always entirely conscious. For example, in order to urinate in the toilet we slip into a mild form of meditation. It is the reason why creative thoughts come when we are in mindless activities. In addition, the writing tasks become increasingly complex.

In order to write well, one must be well read. Thus, literature may be used to stimulate creative thought. Thus, a short passage describing a character is read to the group. Workshop participants are asked to look up, just above eye level, and use their mind's eye to visualize what is being read. Afterwards, students are asked, "Describe someone you know." The question may be more specific, such as, "Describe someone you know in a similar situation."

EXERCISE: Read the beginning paragraphs of the first chapter, *Stone of Scone*, from <u>Richard III: White Boar</u>. After each paragraph look up. Focus just above eye level, and try visualizing what has just been read.

Stone of Scone, the ancient speaking stone, found its way to Westminster Abbey as a triumph of the spoils of war. The Stone had once served as Jacob's pillow at Bethal where Jacob was given a visionary dream. He saw his progeny spreading across the earth and ruling as kings up until the time of the Jews return to the Promised Land. When he awoke, Jacob anointed the Stone with holy oil and set it up as an altar in the Great Temple.

In 602 BC, Nabuchadnezzar and the Babylons sacked Jerusalem. Jeremiah and two women of King David's lineage managed to escape with the Stone to Syria. The Stone was later transported from Syria to Egypt, and through Sicily and Spain to Ireland, where Saint Patrick blessed it. In Ireland the Stone found another name, *Lia Fail.* When a rightful King of Ireland stepped upon it, the Stone sang. The song was akin to a mountain's bellowing roar, rising from its cavernous bowels up through its deepest crevasses.

When an Irish King lost his holiness, by ordering a man killed in a church, the Stone was brought to Dunaad in Scotland to serve as the coronation throne for the Scottish kings. Restlessly, the Stone moved to Iona and then Scone. For more than a thousand years, the Stone of Destiny fulfilled an ancient prophecy:

Except old seers do feign,
And wizard wits be blind,
The Scots in place must reign,
Where they this stone shall find.

EXERCISE: Write down a description and the history of an object that is known to you. It may be a personal item or something you once saw in a museum.

The suggestion is always to write about something, some event or person that is familiar. In order to write believably, one must write about what one knows. Situations, characters and settings may be from the physical world or the non-ordinary

232

world of the Shaman. George Eliot's most successful novels took place in familiar territory. In <u>Adam Bede</u>, George Eliot utilized a story told to her by her aunt, Elizabeth Evans, as well as her father's memories of his childhood. Authors who write good historical fiction, the kind where the reader feels him/herself there, more than likely lived in that place and time.

Some people have never had the experience of thinking creatively. It is as if the left brain has a monopoly on the entire thinking process. For these people it is especially important that their left brain recognize the validity of right brain thought. In the process of doing the exercises, something usually clicks.

EXAMPLE: A young woman (we'll call her Nancy) in one Creativity Class either questioned what she received or applied her left brain to every task at hand.

INSTUCTOR: If everyone in the class concurs, I will lead a group past life regression (Nancy's class was agreeable). In past life regressions I guide the members of the group back to a lifetime that is blocking the creative flow in the current lifetime. The past life regression is like an etheric postmortem. Towards the end of the past life regression, I will say, "Go to the last day of your life. Know that you may rise above the situation. ... What's happening? ... Who's with you? ... Watch the dying process! ... What angel, what loved one is coming to help you cross over? ... Ask them what the lesson of that lifetime was! ... Ask the angels to send healing to you and to all you considered friends, family and enemies in that lifetime! ... Go into the Light with the angels and those loved ones who are your spiritual guides for this journey!"

Afterwards, I ask students to write down specific experiences or a general description of their experiences. After each person shares, what s/he has written, I will check to make sure that at the end of the past life regression that everyone went into the Light. If they didn't, I have them go back into their minds to see themselves after death. I then ask the angels to open the vortex and invite the personality to take the hand of an angel and step into the Light. People oftentimes feel a release or they feel a general sense of peace or well-being come over them. They open up!

Nancy went into a lifetime where she might well be described as a medieval hit man, who truly enjoyed his occupation. After watching herself butcher the last unsuspecting target, Nancy decided that she would become a monk and recreate herself in that lifetime. The problem for Nancy was that she missed out on an opportunity to forgive herself and others, and move on.

For Nancy's sake, I tried the exercise that sends some Shamanic students to the floorboards kicking and screaming — Readings from the Otherworlds without knowing the question or even who is asking the question. When it was Nancy's turn to describe the answer she received, she went on about a golden pyramid. Afterwards, she read the question and found out it was my question about my horses. She dropped her mouth open wide and spoke. "Actually, I initially thought it was a golden horse's ear, not a pyramid." After that Nancy trusted the inspiration she received and allowed it to develop.

As blockages that are within Nancy and the workshop attendees are being released, transformed and healed, it is time to go to the next the core issue and root it out. The following symbol was given to me quite by accident. All I knew at the time was that it helped to release negative relationship patterns. I also knew that it was quite powerful, and that there was more to it. So, I asked God to tell me more.

SYMBOL OF RELEASE: If you wish to draw it try sketching both the triangle and circle counterclockwise (movement of release). Draw the lines left to right from the top down.

David Durok had this to say regarding the symbol for RELEASE, and it seems to fit perfectly: "When someone works with this symbol, it releases the cause of self-destructive behavior by releasing the memory that causes negative patterns to repeat. Damaging blueprints harmfully impact our lives, our relationships, and us. This symbol brings up the memory for us to look at. It is then our choice as to whether we

go into denial, continue to blame others, or work through and release the memory and patterns of self-destruction."
David Durok
Scotland

EXPERIENCE OF CHRISTOPHER CANE OF SOUTHAMPTON, ENGLAND: I drew the symbol for RELEASE from the Fall 2005 Newsletter for a friend of mine, and we both saw the most amazing rainbow light coming from it. Then the light entered my friend's body and aura. She felt it reach deep into the dark areas of her mind and being . . . the ones that held fear and heartache. It was totally amazing to watch her aura shift, change and expand. Then the higher beings had me drain her aura. (Pain Drain used in Touch for Health.) She let go of all the dark gooey stuff, which came to the surface. Then we filled the void with cobalt blue light and then sealed it with gold. It was very interesting.

COMMENT OF CLAIRE CAMPBELL OF ATLANTA, GEORGIA: I feel that the energy of this symbol was at one time held within three symbols. Spirit gave these symbols to a man, who assumed that they were symbols of initiation. He didn't ask what they were to be used for. Too often, people try to fit what they get from spirit into their own box or perceptions of how things are. When they do this they remain stuck in a realm of limited observations, and closed off to greater possibilities.

EXERCISE: The workshop attendees are shown the symbol for RELEASE and then guided into meditation with the suggestion to become small and explore the energy of the

236

symbol. Some people play on the horizontal lines, like a teeter-totter, and investigate the shapes and experience the energy. Others find that they are only able to traverse the perimeters, or are only able to go into the circle but not the triangle. Afterwards the class writes down what happened, those who had difficulties are helped to work through their blockages.

(Examples of working with the symbol for RELEASE have been in previous chapters. This proved to be a good symbol to work with in the Creativity Class as it helped to release and heal blockages to creativity.)

In the fall of 2005, I stayed at Griff Hotel in Warwickshire. It is attached to George Eliot's home, which is now a restaurant. Of this I was completely unaware until Ted Parsons, one of the students in the Creativity Class, pointed it out. The only quote that I had brought to the class was one written by George Eliot (Mary Ann Evans). It is the subtitle of this book. George Eliot is the author of eight novels, including <u>Silas Marner</u> and <u>Middlemarch</u>. Here are some of the exercises and class writings by individuals in the Warwickshire Creativity class:

EXERCISE: Read the description of Ludlow Castle from <u>Richard III: White Boar</u>. After each paragraph look up. Focus just above eye level, and visualize what has just been read.

Ludlow Castle, a massive defensible fortress, stood on high

ground, guarded by both the rivers Tene and Corve, with steep cliffs to the north and west. Built from limestone, quarried from its own site, it was the most strategic fortification on the Welsh boarders. The Norman gatehouse and the battlements on the outer bailey wall were the first glimpses of the castle the party saw as they rode through the town. The Duke was notified immediately that his wife and younger sons had arrived. He breathed an audible sigh of relief, but the seriousness of the moment yet predominated his typical jovial temperament.

Once through the gatehouse they entered the large, four-acre outer bailey or courtyard. Troopes were trained, exercised and mustered in the outer bailey. Horses were grazed and the stables, workshops, lodgings and storehouses were conveniently located here. The Chapel of St. Peter, built by Roger Mortimer, was to the left.

When the Duke and Duchess were in residence, the grounds swarmed with visiting nobles and officials, priests, monks and friars, chambermaids, cooks, clerks, grooms and farriers, weavers and herbalists, tutors, clerks and porters. Some resided in the castle. Others lived in the nearby village.

Holy days and saints' feast days of the liturgical calendar were celebrated in the outer bailey with jousting tournaments and other competitive entertainment. On May Day, each young maiden chose a knight and crowned him with a rosary of roses. At Christmas the Festival of Fools was held. One jester was chosen to serve as a bogus bishop. He was ordained in ridiculously decorative vestments. To the amusement of the crowds, he delivered his sermon in gibberish and sang boorish songs. Midsummer's Eve and Harvest sported special events particular to the occasion.

The U-shaped Mortimer's Tower was unlike the other square towers. It served as the gatehouse that controlled the rear exit from the Castle. It led to Dirham Bridge, which offered the shortest means to Wigmore and Wales. Mortimer's Tower stood nearly directly across from the party on the western perimeter wall. The party proceeded to the Norman gatehouse guarding the inner bailey. Above the entrance to the inner bailey was a carved set of arms.

The inner bailey wall was six feet thick, surrounded by a steep ditch cut out from the rock and flanked by four open-backed, square towers. These were constructed so that archers would be able to send their arrows into anyone attempting to scale the wall. Upon entering the inner bailey, the round Chapel of Saint Mary Magdalene, constructed in the manner of the Knights Templar, stood in front of the party. Its beautifully carved entrance and decorative work invited penitents and worshipers into the circular nave.

The North Range, directly opposite the gatehouse, was built in a crescent shape. Within its walls could be found the Great Hall, measuring 60 by 30 feet. Tapestries hung on the walls. Rush mats were laid on the floors - stone flags on the ground floor and wooden floorboards on the upper floors. Throughout the year, sweet and pungent herbs were sprinkled on the mats and hung from the ceilings to cut obnoxious ordors. All of the mats throughout the castle were removed at the end of May, and replaced by fresh ones.

The kitchen was located within the walls of the North Range. It was busy yearlong, feeding castle residents and preparing feasts for huge banquets. Two of the three fireplaces were large enough to stand in. One measured 16 feet in length and was used to roast meats - large joints and flanks. Whole pigs were secured on spits and turned by young boys. The other fireplace was used for cooking vegetables, pottages and boiling meats.

The bread oven door was held in place with a piece of dough while bread was cooking so that the cook could tell by looking at it when the pastries and breads were ready. Chimneys ran the full height of the North Range wall. The kitchen heat was so intense that only men worked in the kitchen, and they wore little or nothing. Within the walls of the large chimneys were bricks that jutted out and served as footholds so that the chimney sweeps might clean the soot out. A small fireplace provided the pilot fire. Portable charcoal burners were used for frying and grilling.

Meats were butchered and hung in the game room. Open barrels of stone ale, mead and wine were kept in the buttery. The stock was stored in the wine cellar.

Most of the food preparation was carried on at tables in the middle of the kitchen. Assistant cooks helped the head cook and scullions scrubbed the pots and pans. The head cook was in charge of ordering goods and supplies.

The Great Tower, a four-story tall structure immediately to the west of the gatehouse, faced south. It had its own smaller walled courtyard and served as the castle's keep. On the first floor, a two-story living hall and adjoining bedroom provided quarters for the Duke and Duchess when they were in residence. Interiors were decorated with paneling, plasterwork and large tapestries. Fireplaces in each of the rooms provided warmth. Meals for the family and visiting friends or dignitaries were prepared in a smaller kitchen within the keep. Even though the fortress was in the frontier, Ludlow's keep was warmer than most castles.

EXERCISE: Describe a place that you are familiar with. Here are Ted Parsons' first written impressions:

WRITING OF TED PARSONS OF BEDWORTH, ENGLAND: I regard the land around the Mawddach Estuary in Wales as God's Country; my heart feels at home there, Cadair Idris looms over me, protects me, the estuary flows to the sea, the buzzard mews, and below in the valley the train rumbles over the bridge. I can hear the silence. In this land I am at home with my life, my loved one and with myself.

The Lakes are still, the Mountains proud and the Estuary forgiving. The light always changes, the silence is so loud.

I am happy for my ashes to be here, let them fall into the head of the waterfall where I washed the mud away from my heart.

To love and to be loved is enough because there is no limit to love.

EXERCISE: Read the description of Edward II from <u>Richard III: White Boar</u>. After each paragraph look up. Focus just above eye level, and visualize what has just been read.

Lack luster so adequately defined and meticulously delineated Edward II's character that he might well have invented the phrase. Above average in height, strapping, flaxen-haired and handsome, Edward's outward appearance proved to be an empty husk. Ambitionless with regards to military conquest, he also had little interest in matters of state! His major aspiration and preoccupation as king was the enrichment of himself and his friends. He avoided at all costs any sport associated with kings, preferring instead menial, energy-efficient tasks and hobbies.

It was not Edward's fault that he inherited a treasury, exhausted from years of war and a populace, discontented with the resulting burdens of high taxes. Edward, however, added to his difficulties by frequently antagonizing feudal magnates. After losing the Battle of Bannockburn to the Scottish, who fought under the leadership of Robert Bruce, the Scots ravaged northern England unopposed. Rather than engage the Scots in combat, the governing body of lords, led by Thomas of Lancaster, fought against the King's party. Only through the efforts of the noble Earl of Pembroke were the two feuding factions reconciled.

The dysfunctional kingdom would have been put straight were it not for Edward II's insistence on absolute rule. An additional rub to the lords was that he depended on the advise of only two men, whom he showered with riches. Edward had not learned his lesson! He had not changed his ways!

All in all, Edward II was nobody's idea of a proper medieval king. His queen, Isabella, detested Edward most of all - so much so, that she and her lover, Roger Mortimer of Wigmore, arranged to have the King detained and murdered. Hoping to make it look as if Edward had died of natural causes, a hot poker was rammed up into his bowels. While the deed was carried out surreptitiously in Berkeley Castle, suspicions and rumors circulated throughout the realm. An English bard christened Isabella the she-wolf of France. Undaunted, Isabella piously attended her late husband's funeral. Afterwards, she happily assumed her new role as Queen Dowager of England.

As a couple, Edward and Isabella had been incongruously mismatched. As king, Edward had been unpopular among lords and commons alike. Who could have predicted that from Edward II's loins would arise a king by whom all future English kings would be measured?

EXERCISE: Describe someone you are familiar with.

WRITING OF TED PARSONS OF BEDWORTH, ENGLAND: Do You, Do You, Do You want to dance … or … Dancing With George Eliot
(in the garden at Griff House)

She took me to her garden and asked me what I wanted; I said that I really want to dance, with you. I danced with her in the sunlit garden, her dress was blue, we spun around. Funny really, I had always pictured George Eliot as a rather dour character and now here she was with me in her beautiful late summer garden. Bees buzzing on the lavender. I want to stay here, stay in a new light.
I answered from my heart and I was surprised by the answer and now I saw George Eliot in a new light; and that she could make me feel it was ok to dance in her garden. All because I spoke from my heart.
I so admired what she said about it being never too late to be the person you always wanted to be. So much generosity in the life, so much grace, always a chance. The infinite gifts of the universe. Always our choice, my opportunity to feel my heart, to feel my passion, to stay in the new light of dance. To dance, to swim, to be alive now.

I can still smell the flowers, feel the joy of that dance, savoir my glimpse of George Eliot and what she meant to me in her garden; in that light, that scent, the warm touch of her hands and her waist as we danced.

A return to passion and gratitude.

As she came alive for me so did Warwickshire and Bedworth. I had judged so much in the past but now I was free to receive the abundance of gifts. I recalled a conversation from when I lived here in the seventies: "If only you could step out of your front door and see that you were in the Universe as well as the street." So I stepped out and my perception was changed, my eyes opened.

Feel with my heart
Learn to feel
It is time for passion
time for the heart
Listen to the teacher
Be open …

Because of the prejudice against women, Mary Ann Evans was forced to write under a pen name — George Eliot. Though she died in the later part of the 19th century, well before Ted Parsons was born, she visited the Creativity Class in Bedworth. Personality does survive death! It is possible for the departed to assist the living. There is a potential in meditative states to glean more understanding; Ted obviously found more.

Ted added this concerning the class: "I am so glad I met you and want to thank you for the inspiration and healing you brought to me. I will continue the writing and I intend to start painting again. I want to do something with both paint and words."

Writing lovely, inspirational prose and poetry is not the only objective of creative thought. Once the mind is clear, blockages are released and the channel from the top of the head to the center of the brain is clear, other aspects of imaginative thinking are possible. Inventive solutions to both personal and professional quandaries may be found. John Ostrowskis found the cosmic garbage disposal unit:

WRITING OF JOHN OSTROWSKIS, THE CLINIC, SHEFFIELD, ENGLAND: One particular meditation experience was dear and deep, I remembered it particularly as it seemed to make no sense. On an exercise to connect the head to the heart, I immediately began to see the bones of my left hand, which was palm down on my thigh. From this starting point a white laser light began moving from the thumb side of the middle finger from the nail bed to the joint of the metacarpal phalanges, and back and forth. A short while later, I saw my heart beat in my left hand. With this came an incredibly deep peaceful relaxation. A message of, "You can do this yourself by visualizing this scene!" came to me. As with all good things, I neglected it for a couple of weeks, then remembered the exercise. At times it feels like it connects me to a cosmic garbage disposal unit, removing aspects of darkness in my energies, at times it seems far more refined and tunes me to something more than myself. Due to the simplicity and mainly to the fact that the exercise WORKS for me, I have been doing it daily before work. I have far more mental

and physical energy, a greater sense of discernment and am attracting a more positive experience of life.
John Ostrowskis

INSTRUCTOR: Energetically, the middle finger connects to the heart. It is particularly sensitive in that many people are unable to wear metal rings on middle fingers. The other aspect of John's exercise deals with the feminine and masculine. The feminine, right, creative brain controls the left side of the physical body. Thus, when someone does this exercise with the middle finger of the left hand they are releasing and healing issues concerning women or female issues. The masculine, left, logical brain controls the right side of the physical body. When the exercise is done with the middle finger of the right hand then issues concerning men or masculine issues are released and healed.

John also added this concerning the class: "The whole workshop was a remarkable day for me. I received a tremendous amount of healing. I left a truckload of dark energy behind and have my own personalized home exercise to continue with. All of the whilst enjoying the company of a group, which bonded immediately. A fantastic experience."

EXERCISE: The subtitle of this book, It's Never Too Late To Be Who You Might Have Been, is used in the second Shamanic class as the theme for a journey.

INSTRUCTOR: When I begin beating the drum you will see yourself clearly in your mind's eye standing in a beautiful place in nature. You will find a way to the Underworld. When you reach the Underworld you will call upon a nature spirit to assist you. If you are taken to the Upperworld, an angel will guide you. Ask to be shown your path of life, the plan you helped to create before you were born. It may be shown to you figuratively or symbolically. If you are off your path, ask, "How may I live the life I was meant to live?" You may ask questions. Simply watch yourself and see what happens.

If you are already on your path ask, "Help me to become the person I was always meant to be." Again, you may ask questions. Simply watch yourself and see what happens. The answers you receive may be anything from crystal clear to cloaked in metaphors.

When I change the beat of the drum, it is time to come back. If you are in the middle of something please finish what you are doing and then come back. You will return the same way you went down.

EXPERIENCE OF WILLEM BOEREN OF THE NETHERLANDS: I came to a beautiful place. I looked back to see if the blackness was still behind me. It was gone. Eagle and Wolf asked me, "Why don't you trust?"

Eagle had a much bigger fish and wolf had a much bigger rabbit. When I asked what they were for, I received the same answer I had received on the journey to the Underworld. They told me that there was more for me. So, I asked God, "Show me!"

Merlin appeared and then I became Merlin with white wings. The wings became gold. Dust fell off the wings. When the wings were dusted, the dust was transformed and fell to the earth as diamonds.

I climbed up the pyramid. The entrance was guarded by the Buddha with a ruby in his 3rd eye. He sat there! Surrounding Buddha was a wealth beyond measure. However, I was told that the large ruby has to remain on Buddha. The ruby is like the golden goose that supplies diamonds and other jewels. If the goose is killed or the ruby comes off Buddha, the source of wealth is stamped out. A woman came and together we distributed the jewels to humanity. There was plenty for everyone, but the wealth was to be used well.

EXPERIENCE OF MARIAN VALKENBURGH OF THE NETHERLANDS: I asked, "How may I become the person I was always meant to be? How am I to live the life I was always meant to live?"

I saw myself outside the city as a teacher. All that I taught concerned energy and how to use it. All of the people, including myself, had auras that I could see. The more that I taught, the shinier I became.

An elephant came. The elephant became shiny and white, and then it turned into stone. When I asked why, I was told that this was a symbol of strength for me.

I went up and disappeared.

EXPERIENCE OF JOAO RAMOS OF PORTUGAL: I went down. I was there with the power animals. We were in the mountains of Spain and Portugal. Then I was at a river with a large boat. While I was speaking with the animals a camel came. I asked him what he was doing there. He said, "I belong here."

I went onto the boat and we were going up the river. Then I was on the beach watching again. Then there were two boats, but the river did not have enough room for both boats. Then you stopped drumming.

INSTRUCTOR: When the drum stops, you always have the option to stay in the Otherworlds and work things out. The class will be quiet until everyone opens their eyes. The next time you journey, you may go back with the intention of finding out why there were two boats in a river that was too small for them both. There are two obvious reasons, but keep in mind that the Otherworlds are not bound to the logic of this one. The first is that you have determined your life's path, but the Universe has another. Thus, one of the boats has to go. The second is that you have a dual path and the river requires widening.

You may also do 'problem solving in your dreamstate'. (Discussed in Reiki & Other Rays of Touch Healing) When you go to bed at night and close your eyes, state your question clearly in your mind, using as few words as possible. The question maybe, "Why two boats in a river too small?" Keep repeating the same question, using the same words, over and over again until you fall asleep.

In the morning you will receive your answer. If you don't receive your answer on the following morning, keep doing it at night until the answer comes. Also know that the answer may come during the day in some unexpected and surprising way.

EXPERIENCE OF ANDRE BEUKERS OF THE NETHERLANDS: I went down the roots of the World Tree and met my power animals. I asked the question. The power animals took me to the angels and told me to ask again. The angels asked me, "Will you trust us?"

I answered, "Yes!"

Buddha asked, "Can you give your heart to God?"

I said, "Yes!"

Then I saw a lot of gold and purple light.

EXERCISE: On the East Coast of the United States there were Native American Crow Shaman who were able to shape-shift. There were also Hopi who had this ability. The following is from Tera, My Journey Home: Alternative Healing.

Some Shaman were so attuned that they could shape-shift and become their tribal totem. Other tribes were able to psychically manipulate the elemental forces that comprised their tribal totem. Shaman developed their psychic abilities through careful observation and harmonic interaction with nature. Shamanic gifts that are birthed and nurtured in one lifetime may take form in a new way in another lifetime.

Shape-shifting in the physical begins with a heightened awareness of the physical body. *(Super-awareness of the physical body is the beginning of any supernatural event involving the physical body — invisibility, teleporting, vision quest, etc. The physical foundation for using the physical body psychically involves exercise and eating healthy food.)* Then there is realization that there is a vertical shift in the solar plexus. Quite suddenly this etheric rod moves or shifts to the side and the physical form changes.

It is called shape-shifting, not shape-transformation. All animals have exactly the same bones and muscles that humans have. In each species, bones and muscles may be shortened, lengthened, combined or at a slightly different angle. To shape-shift, the bones and muscles re-adjust. For example, for a human to shift into a four-legged, one of the sensations is that the shoulder blades and arms shift downwards. In contrast, for a human to shift into a winged, the shoulder blades shift backwards. Could it be that evolution is God's Master Plan?

One benefit to shape-shifting in the Otherworlds is to gain the perspective of another creature. To discover attributes and what each species contributes. Shape-shifting in the Otherworlds is also a way to think outside of ordinary limitations. To step outside of the box!

INSTRUCTOR: When I begin beating the drum you will see yourself clearly in your mind's eye standing in a beautiful place in nature. You will find a way to the Underworld. When you reach the Underworld you will call upon a power animal to assist you. Ask the power animal, "How might I change my shape so that I resemble you?" They might answer your question directly or take you to the angels. Or you may find you go directly to the angels. However and wherever you go, know that it is where you will find your answers.

EXPERIENCE OF WILLEM BOEREN OF THE NETHERLANDS: It happened quickly. The stairs in the World Tree were larger than I had remembered. I came out and onto eagle's back. We flew off. I asked, "Please help me to shape-shift into a bird."

He told me that I could do it myself. I turned into a bird and flew on the wind. We flew to the angels. I asked again how to shape-shift. The angels told me to try. First I became a human, then a wolf, lion and tiger. Then I asked, "Why am I only these kinds of animals?"

I turned into a mouse and asked, "Why?"

The angels responded, "Mice are able to go to places that other animals cannot go. Though they are small in small places, they hear things that others do not have the opportunity to hear."

I asked the angels, "What is the good of shape-shifting?"

"So you can feel what the animal feels and use the power of the animal."

Then I became a giraffe so that I could scan the whole surroundings. Then an eagle so that I could see sharply! Then a gorilla, who was aggressive and strong! When I became an elephant I had the power to take down walls or build bridges.

EXPERIENCE OF MARIAN VALKENBURGH OF THE NETHERLANDS: Shape-shifting went quickly. When I was a wolf I became aware of the movement of the wolf. When I was a shark I could feel the water. Then I became a whale. I felt the strength of the whale and dove deep into the ocean. I turned into an eagle and felt freedom. I was soaring and had the ability to look over and above situations. I became a horse and I ran and ran. At all times, the small, white, shiny, stone elephant was with me.

EXPERIENCE OF JOAO RAMOS OF PORTUGAL:
I went down to the power animals. I changed
into a hummingbird, and was surprised that
I could do that. Then I became a falcon.
Suddenly, I was in front of Buddha. He told
me that I had to meditate more.

I was shown a big stone door that I
had to go through to get to the angels. It
opened easily when I pushed it. An angel
greeted me. I asked him, "How can I
change?"

He took me to a large bath with green,
translucent water. I went into the water
and my head went under three or four times.
I stepped out of the water. The angel dried
me off. Then I tried shape-shifting.

First I became a dog. Then into a
wolf, who had lots of energy. I wanted to
jump everywhere.

EXPERIENCE OF ANDRE BEUKERS OF THE
NETHERLANDS: I climbed into the World Tree
and climbed up. At the third branch an
angel came and asked, "Where are you
going?"

I answered, "To see the angels!"

He said, "You don't have to go
further. I am here."

I asked, "How do I shape-shift?"

"Your mind is tired. Rest! When you
need to shape-shift you will be able to do
it. You've done it before!"

I slept until the drum called me back.

EXERCISE: To become invisible: One
would focus on the physical body and
imagine all of the cells turning and facing
the same direction. In this way, space is
created between the cells so that people
can see through the space.

Katimbo

or Ama Deus

Alberto Aguas brought Ama Deus (I Love God) to the United States. It is sacred healing and has been used for thousands upon thousands of years by the Guarani *(Gau ra nee)* Tribe or los Guaranis located deep in the central jungle of Brazil. The problem is that Alberto did not teach the whole system in any one place.

The spirit of Alberto Aguas guided me to a man who had gathered together the entire Ama Deus system. Later, while teaching a class in New York City, I discovered that the instructor in the next classroom had studied with Alberto on several occasions. When I showed her the Ama Deus notes that I had retyped, she confirmed that it was all in order.

I had no intention of putting Ama Deus into a book until I found out that people were changing the symbols. In some cases, making them extremely complicated. Other people were charging many thousands of dollars, which they never had to pay for Ama Deus. Alberto's spirit came to me again requesting that I include Ama Deus in <u>Tera, My Journey Home</u> so that his life's work would continue to have meaning.

In 2005, a woman from Brazil emailed me, asking a simple question, "Do you believe that Alberto Aguas was protecting the Shamanic healing system you call Ama Deus?"

When people ask me a question the answer comes. Not always right away, but it does come. In this case the answer was very clear that Alberto had protected Ama Deus. She responded, "Right answer!" She then proceeded to tell me that the Guarani call the Ama Deus Shamanic system Katimbo. There is a lot in a name, and Katimbo resonates strongly with the system.

This chapter includes Katimbo and how to use it. It is more inclusive because understanding has come through using Katimbo. Thus, the directions are simpler; however, the meaning remains the same.

Katimbo is both easy to use and offers good visualization practice. The Shaman also has the opportunity to patiently watch to see what the spiritual forces will do. When the simple rules are observed Katimbo works.

Like good governments or a well-organized classroom, Katimbo has only a few good rules: 1) As with all Shamanic work, the objective is set prior to the actual practice or journey. 2) Katimbo does not work with evil intentions. Should an individual try to do so, the spirit guides and energy of Katimbo will disappear. 3) Katimbo symbols are not to be intentionally changed. 4) Once the system is opened, no other symbols are brought into the practice. 5) If the Shaman wants to use other symbols, then Katimbo must be closed before other symbols are used. PLEASE READ THE LAST PAGE OF THIS CHAPTER *(pages 274)* TO LEARN HOW TO CLOSE KATIMBO.

Love moves mountains and creates an environment conducive for healing and divination. Thus, the Shaman focuses her/his breath upon her/his heart —

256

breathing in love and exhaling compassion. In the mind's eye the Shaman visualizes the love that is being created. Using the word, Katimbo, as a mantra independent of the breath, the Shaman begins to feel the presence of angels, higher beings,

Symbol One is imprinted on the **left palm.** How? Visualize Symbol One, at the same time concentrating on the palm of the left hand for one minute. If the image of Symbol One disappears from the third eye, open your eyes, look at the symbol and close your eyes again. Interestingly enough, you will feel as though Symbol One is being drawn on the left palm in a series of electrical dots. The left hand feels bigger.

What is the purpose of Symbol One? The symbols that are used in the healing and divination work seem to 'ride in' on the energy wave of Symbol One.

1.

Symbol Two is imprinted on the **right palm** in exactly the same manner. Again the feeling of electrical dots will be experienced in the right palm and the hand will feel larger.

What is the purpose of Symbol Two? The two horizontal lines of Symbol Two serve to anchor or ground the other Katimbo symbols, which are used in the Shamanic work.

2.

_____

_____

Healing & divination work: Once the system is opened and the intention has been set, other Katimbo symbols that are appropriate to accomplishing the goal, may be visualized one at a time. The idea is to visualize the symbol and watch to see what happens. It is helpful to visualize symbols just above the imaginary horizon line in your mind's eye. Concentrated, focused attention is the key to Katimbo.

Be patient and be kind to yourself! If the mind's eye loses the symbol completely, simply open your eyes, look at the symbol for one minute and close your eyes once again. As you watch a symbol, it may change into something else. You may ask questions. While the Katimbo symbols do not have specific colors, they may change into a color.

It is helpful to begin with Symbol Nine, which is used to call in spiritual guide(s) to carry out the work.

Symbol Nine may also be used to bring in a new **spiritual guide** for oneself. Symbol Nine is never sent to another person.

Symbol Nine is used to call upon the spiritual guide(s) that will help with the particular healing or divination at hand. After breathing love and imprinting Symbols

258

One and Two, visualize Symbol Nine and watch to see who comes in.

After calling in the spirit guide(s) continue by using Katimbo symbols appropriate to the goal.

9.

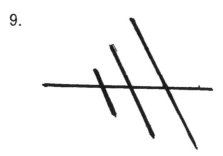

Symbol Ten may be used for **self-healing.** After doing the spiritual practice, which includes breathing love and imprinting Symbols One and Two, and using Symbol Nine to bring in spirit guide(s), visualize Symbol Ten. Try scooping Symbol Ten into your heart with your physical hands as you visualize it in your mind's eye. Or watch Symbol Ten and see what happens. Symbol Ten may go to a visualization of yourself. Or you may not understand the visual metaphors.

10.

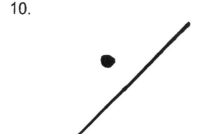

Symbol Six is used to rescue a **dying person**. If it is their time to go, Symbol Six helps the dying to work out karma and aids in a peaceful transition. If it is not time for the dying person to go, Symbol Six helps in the **healing** process.

Visualize Symbol Six and breathe it out to the person's heart. It may be done in person or absentee. If absentee, send symbol in the golden ball of light, which is Symbol Three.

If the person is present, use your thumb and third finger of both hands. Using a feather-like touch, put the third finger on top of the second toe at the base of the toe and the thumb under the toe at the base of the toe. Do this with both hands. After breathing love and imprinting Symbols One and Two, and using Symbol Nine to bring in spirit guide(s), visualize Symbol Six and breathe it up to the person's heart.

You may repeat this three days in a row or until there is a change.

6.

Symbol Three is a brilliant ball of golden light (if another color comes in, it is what is required). After breathing love and imprinting Symbols One and Two, and using Symbol Nine to bring in spirit guide(s), visualize the golden ball and watch to see what happens. Or you may place Katimbo symbol(s) in the golden ball and say, "To ___*(name of person, place or event)*___ !"

3.

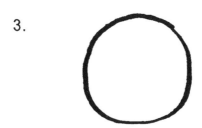

Symbol Seven is used for those who have been **dead for less than 21 days** to help them to travel speedily to the Light. If it has been longer, use Symbol Eight. It is typically a good idea to light a white candle and burn it when working with ghosts.

If you are working with the body, hold the second toe between your thumb and third finger as described above. After breathing love and imprinting Symbols One and Two, and using Symbol Nine to bring in spirit guide(s), visualize Symbol Seven going into the feet, up through the body and out the top of the head. Watch to see what happens.

When you feel, see or hear the deceased, ask the angels to open the Vortex of Light. Encourage the deceased to take the hand of an angel and go into the Light.

When Symbol Seven is used absentee, it may be sent within the golden ball of Symbol Three. Symbol Seven may be used for 21 days after death.

7.

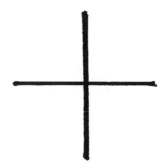

Symbol Eight is used to **send earthbound spirits to the Light**. After breathing love and imprinting Symbols One and Two, and using Symbol Nine to bring in spirit guide(s), visualize Symbol Eight. If you cannot see, hear or feel the spirit of the departed, place Symbol Eight in the golden ball of Symbol Three. If the soul has materialized do not use Symbol Three.

Ask the angels to open the Vortex of Light and encourage the deceased to take the hand of an angel and go into the Light. When Symbol Eight is used absentee, it may be sent within the golden ball of Symbol Three.

8.

Symbol Twenty-Three is used as **protection** during exorcisms. After breathing love and imprinting Symbols One and Two, and using Symbol Nine to bring in spirit guide(s), visualize Symbol Twenty-Three over the heads of observers in the room, including animals, and yourself. It does not go over the head of the healee. After the exorcism, Symbol Twenty-Three is the last thing that the Shaman sees. It is not sent to the Light in Symbol Four *(page 274).*

23.

Symbol Twenty-Two is used for **exorcisms** after everyone else in the room receives Symbol Twenty-Three over their heads. In order for any healing to take place, the possessed individual must give her/his consent to the exorcism.

Hold the second toe between your thumb and third finger as described with Symbols Six and Seven. After breathing love and imprinting Symbols One and Two, and using Symbol Nine to bring in spirit guide(s), visualize Symbol Twenty-Two going into the feet, up through the body and out the top of the head. Watch to see what happens.

Exorcisms take a bit of time — an hour or several hours. After the entity is released use Symbol Eight to send the entity or entities to the Light. Follow the directions for Symbol Eight.

Again, the last thing the Shaman sees is Symbol Twenty-Three.

If the entity is having a difficult time leaving, close Katimbo *(page 274)* and use the symbol for RELEASE *(page 235)*. Stop using RELEASE if you reopen Katimbo.

22.

Symbol Thirteen is used for animals — four-legged, winged, etc. After breathing love and imprinting Symbols One and Two, and using Symbol Nine to bring in spirit guide(s), visualize Symbol Thirteen.

13.

Symbol Twelve may be used in an **emergency** when many people who know the Katimbo symbols are gathered together. After breathing love and imprinting Symbols One and Two, and using Symbol Nine to bring in spirit guide(s), visualize Symbol Twelve. If everyone is sitting in a circle, pass Symbol Twelve around the circle in a counterclockwise direction to release, or clockwise to bring in energy.

12.

Symbol Eleven is also used in an **emergency** but without the spiritual practice. Symbol Eleven represents spirals that are drawn from the center outwards by drawing the symbol in the air with both arms and hands. Spirals maybe drawn clockwise or counterclockwise. (Perhaps, counterclockwise with the left arm and clockwise with the right arm.) In this manner a lot of energy is created. If working with a group of people, stand in a circle. Make certain that there is enough space between members of the group. Visualize the energy traveling around the group in a counterclockwise direction for release and clockwise to bring energy in.

In an emergency when the Shaman is alone, s/he creates very fast spirals over the healee's head. Then s/he works on the front and back, and then zeroes in on the injured area. Spirals are repeated over and over again.

Symbol Eleven may also be used as the other Katimbo symbols are used. After breathing love and imprinting Symbols One and Two, and using Symbol Nine to bring in spirit guide(s), visualize Symbol Eleven. If the situation or injured person is absent, send Symbol Eleven in the golden ball of Symbol Three. Symbol Eleven may be used on others or oneself.

11.

   Symbol Fourteen is used for **planetary
healing.** After breathing love and imprinting
Symbols One and Two, and using Symbol Nine
to bring in spirit guide(s), visualize
Symbol Fourteen. The golden ball of Symbol
Three is not necessary as we are on Mother
Earth. If, however, energy is intended for a
specific and distant location, Symbol
Fourteen may be placed in Symbol Three's
golden ball.

14.

   Symbol Fifteen is used on **birthdays** —
yours or someone else's. On your birthday
the sun is in the same place in the heavens
as it was the day you were born. In
astrological terms this is called a solar
return. While your natal horoscope is always

a part of you, each year you get a solar return astrology chart, which influences that particular year.

After breathing love and imprinting Symbols One and Two, and using Symbol Nine to bring in spirit guide(s), visualize Symbol Fifteen. If for yourself, scoop it up with your physical hands to your heart. Or watch the symbol to see what happens. If sending it to another person who is absent, send Symbol Fifteen in Symbol Three's golden ball. If the birthday person is present, blow the symbol into her/his heart.

15.

Symbol Sixteen invites **dreams**. It is only used on oneself. After breathing love and imprinting Symbols One and Two, and using Symbol Nine to bring in spirit guide(s), visualize Symbol Sixteen. You may do this before going to sleep and simply visualize the symbol as you nod off.

You may also go through the now familiar spiritual routine and then blow the symbol onto a stone. Place the stone under your pillow and go to sleep. Either way, the symbol helps to bring in knowledge, answers or helps to breakthrough when one feels stuck. Have a paper and pen next to your bed so that you may write your dreams down the following morning. If it doesn't work on the first try, keep trying. It will work!

16.

Symbol Seventeen is used to bring **hidden knowledge into consciousness**. After breathing love and imprinting Symbols One and Two, and using Symbol Nine to bring in spirit guide(s), visualize Symbol Seventeen. Breathe your question and the symbol into the ethers or to the Akashic Records. You may ask specific questions, or "What is useful for me to know at this time?"

Symbol Seventeen may produce recollections and visions from past lives. It is only used on oneself. Symbol Seventeen is called the **mastermind symbol** because it connects to the superconscious.

The difference between working with this symbol and the other symbols may be felt with experience. Symbol Seventeen looks very much like the symbol Algiz from the Runes, which is used for protection. When Symbol Seventeen is used within Katimbo, Symbol Seventeen works to bring in information.

17.

Symbol **Eighteen** is used on **world leaders, world situations** or important causes. After breathing love and imprinting Symbols One and Two, and using Symbol Nine to bring in spirit guide(s), visualize Symbol Eighteen. Symbol Eighteen may also be used with Symbol Fourteen. If the situation is removed, use the golden ball of Symbol Three.

18.

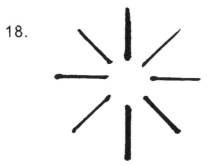

Symbol **Nineteen** is used when other symbols do not fit or there is an **unknown situation.** It may be used on others or oneself. After breathing love and

imprinting Symbols One and Two, and using
Symbol Nine to bring in spirit guide(s),
visualize Symbol Nineteen. Watch the symbol
to see what occurs.

19.

    Symbol Twenty is used on **other
people's hearts** and **healing others.** After
breathing love and imprinting Symbols One
and Two, and using Symbol Nine to bring in
spirit guide(s), visualize Symbol Twenty.
If used absentee, send Symbol Twenty in
Symbol Three's golden ball. Watch to see
what happens.

20

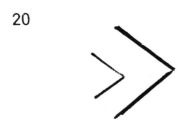

    Symbol Twenty-One is used at the time
of the **full moon** to manifest a particular
thing or bring an answer to a question. It
is important to be clear about request or
question before beginning.
    After breathing love and imprinting
Symbols One and Two, and using Symbol Nine
to bring in spirit guide(s), visualize

Symbol Seventeen and then Symbol Twenty-One. Hold images for one minute (one minute will seem to be a very long time). You may also do this just prior to the full moon, as the energy then is also strong.

21.

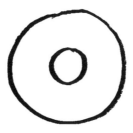

Symbol Twenty-Four is used to find a friend or someone who is missing. It may also be used to send a message to a friend. After breathing love and imprinting Symbols One and Two, and using Symbol Nine to bring in spirit guide(s), visualize Symbol Twenty-Four. Watch to see what happens.

24.

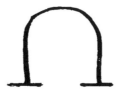

Symbol Twenty-Five is used to help people heal their eyes. It is for both physical and mental vision (inner eye). It may be used on others or oneself. If sent absentee also use Symbol Three.

After breathing love and imprinting Symbols One and Two, and using Symbol Nine to bring in spirit guide(s), visualize Symbol Twenty-Five. Watch to see what happens.

25.

Symbol Twenty-Six is used on newborns up until three months of age. It helps the soul make its transition into the physical body. It has been repeated by psychics or seers through the ages that it is more difficult to be born than it is to die. Death becomes difficult when the spiritual nature of mankind has been ignored or misunderstood.

After breathing love and imprinting Symbols One and Two, and using Symbol Nine to bring in spirit guide(s), visualize Symbol Twenty-Six. Watch to see what happens. The angels know when the baby has had enough.

26.

Symbol Five, like the swirling arm movements of Symbol Eleven, is done without the now very familiar spiritual routine. This symbol **clears**. It may be used over food, medicine, water, beverages, etc. It is used for everything that is put in or on the body. It may be used to remove implants, needles, transplants, germs — anything foreign that has entered the body.

It can take out emotions. For example, when eating in a restaurant, if the cook is having a bad day, her/his emotions affect the food s/he is preparing. It is also possible to remove chlorine from drinking water.

To use Symbol Five you may simply visualize it over whatever is to be ingested or put on the body. It is also possible to touch the fingertips of both hands together and form an upside-down "V" with both hands and your arms. Call upon the angels and other spirit guides to help you to clear. Visualize Symbol Five in your mind's eye and bring your hands and arms down.

5.

Symbol Four is a process that is used to **close Katimbo or Ama Deus healing:** First, Symbol One loops up into a single wave. Second, the two lines of Symbol Two appear within the wave. Third, Symbol Four is closed by visualizing a single horizontal line over the wave. Fourth, Katimbo symbol(s) that have been worked with are placed within the two lines. In the example below, Symbol Thirteen (used for healing animals) is sent back to Source. If several symbols have been used, these may all be placed within Symbol Four and sent back to the Light. As the symbols are released, open your heart and thank God and all the spirits and angels who have helped in the healing, divination or magic work. In this way, the symbols will come back to you stronger the next time you open Katimbo.

4.

Reviews

Reiki & Other Rays of Touch Healing:
Reviewed in Nov/Dec 1994 **The Inner Voice** by
Nancy Rajala:

Cover art is a watercolor painted by
the author. . . . A comprehensive manual
on healing. The author gives concrete
examples in both the use of symbols and a
variety of healing techniques interwoven in
her own healing process (following two
automobile accidents) and her subsequent
work on the inner planes with Sai Baba and
other teachers. The book explains
techniques that can be utilized to develop
psychic abilities and how to achieve deeper
levels of meditation, and then ties this in
with the healing process and different
mysticisms.

Kathleen offers her readers a fresh,
meaningful understanding of the history of
Reiki combined with Jesus' teachings and
related aspects of other spiritualisms.
There are chapters dealing with the use of
healing energy in ceremonial work and Feng
Shui, the Chinese art of altering life
circumstances by altering one's environment.
There's also a chapter devoted to healing
animals, including a story of how a horse
was healed of blindness in two weeks.

Kathleen believes that all healing
energy comes from the Creative, Loving Force
behind this universe, and the final chapter
explains the dynamics of initiation into
rays of healing. If you are a healer, or
you're involved in a healing process, it is

a source you may find yourself often referring to."

Reiki & Other Rays of Touch Healing 5th Edition
Fall 2004 Issue of **Leading Edge Review**

Are you interested in developing your psychic or healing abilities? Going through a healing process? Do you want to understand the phenomenon of spontaneous healing? How do alterative healing methods and techniques work? If Shamanic Journeys and meditation operate in the field of possibilities described in quantum physics, are there specific procedures that aid or hinder the creative process? If so, this still original book may have the answers you seek.

Milner's writing style over the years has evolved into engaging texts that merit savoring as opposed to a quick read. She has an uncanny ability to perceive psychically, which impacts upon her writing, affording her readers the opportunity to observe in a fresh way. Stories and examples of healings are both touching and meaningful. We look forward to her take on Richard III in her soon to be released novel, *White Boar.*

"She's the real deal!" Michael Harrison *Talkers Magazine*

Tera, My Journey Home 2nd edition
Reviewed in March 2000 issue of **Magical Blend** by Kristian Rice

Kathleen Ann Milner is the author of the only two books that are available on Seichem and the aspects of the four elemental healing rays. In her newest edition (second edition) of *Tera, My Journey Home,* she deals with self-healing as a substitute for conventional medical treatment. Her focus is on symptoms, healing energies and the channeling of healing energy, which facilitates self-healing. She has combined Reiki with Buddhist beliefs to unlock this phenomenon. She educates and shares her insights on how to tune into healing and psychic abilities. Readers will find this gem of a book to be an insightful reference to the healing forces hidden within our universe.

Tera, My Journey Home: Alternative Healing
3rd edition
Summer 2004 issue of **Leading Edge Review**

Is your tongue white? Do you wake up tired? Do you have trouble losing or putting on weight? You will discover that the above symptoms are characteristics of secondary infections, which are unresponsive to antibiotics. Milner maps out the whys, hows and practical application of a variety of alternative therapies designed to restore homeostasis for this and other health issues.

Other chapters include a Shamanic & Divination system that may be used by anyone, retraining and therapeutics for abused horses, elemental healing, moving Qi, and healing past lives. Well-written, documented, witnessed accounts and stories of healings, and thought-out examples bestow credibility and meaning.

". . She educates and shares her insights on how to tune into healing and psychic abilities. Readers will find this gem of a book to be an insightful reference to the healing forces hidden within our universe." *2nd edition reviewed in Volume #68 Magical Blend Magazine*

Between Two Worlds; The Story of Henry VIII and Anne Boleyn — and Her Celtic Heritage
Reviewed in **Magical Blend** by Susan Dobra (issue dated June 2004)

Whenever a story is set in a distant time and place and dramatized, as this one is, we usually call it historical fiction. But Kathleen Ann Milner's story of Henry VIII and Anne Boleyn has an interesting claim on historical accuracy. Milner believes she was Boleyn in a past life. She details the evidence for her belief in the second half of this fascinating book, and makes a convincing enough case that the story presented in the first half appears in a whole new light.

We all know the story of King Henry's penchant for lopping off the heads of his wives — Anne Boleyn was the second of six. She is often treated unkindly by historians as a usurper to the queen's throne. Milner sees it differently. She presents Boleyn as a sympathetic figure, and also weaves in the details of her skills in Celtic magic, taught to her by her grandmother. *Between Two Worlds* is a spellbinding book that brings to life Anne Boleyn's precarious place in one of the most treacherous social structures ever to exist. It deftly humanizes the key players and artfully engages the reader with its surprising revelations. If you're interested in what it was really like in the court of Henry VIII, you should read *Between Two Worlds.*

Symbols in Healing: Reiki II
Reviewed in August 1994 **Body Mind Spirit** magazine by Jane Kuhn:

In this video, Kathleen Milner draws and explains the symbols most people are given in Reiki II initiation and goes beyond to explore additional symbols that work to heal. The first symbols that Satya Sai Baba gave her for the purpose of releasing karma and past life issues are shown. Each symbol presented is for a different purpose and for healing a different part of the body. She encourages us to heal the past and create a beautiful life for ourselves in the present.

Healing Hands: Reiki I
Reviewed in August 1994 **Body Mind Spirit** magazine by Jane Kuhn:

Kathleen Milner works from the knowledge that all healing comes from God/Goddess and that we are all capable of channeling, healing and experiencing self-healing. She demonstrates working with touch points on the body to get to the root cause behind pain and disease. Angels and spirit guides are actively engaged in the healing process. She encourages participation of the healees as they share what they are experiencing in their minds and bodies as the healing occurs. Visualization and problem-solving techniques that have been used by great scientists and inventors including Thomas Edison and Albert Einstein are discussed. <u>The video and the healing experience are quite impactful. I experienced them first-hand.</u>